TICKET TO RIDE

The Essential Guide to the World's Greatest Roller Coasters and Thrill Rides

TICKET TO RIDE

The Essential Guide to the World's Greatest Roller Coasters and Thrill Rides

Patrick Hook

CHARTWELL
BOOKS

This edition published in 2019 by Chartwell Books
an imprint of The Quarto Group
142 West 36th Street, 4th Floor
New York, NY 10018 USA
T (212) 779-4972 F (212) 779-6058
www.QuartoKnows.com

© 2019 by Greene Media Ltd.

ISBN: 978-0-7858-3577-6

Printed and bound in China

10 9 8 7 6 5 4 3 2 1

Design: Greene Media Ltd/Eleanor Forty Design

Page 1 "Son of Beast" was a woodie at Kings Island, Cincinnati, OH. Designed by Werner Stengel, it opened on May 26, 2000, taking the world roller coaster height and speed records. It only operated for nine years before being taken out of service in 2009, and was finally demolished in 2012.

Page 2 Liseburg Park in Sweden boasts numerous attractions, one of which is the Norse mythology themed area where "Valkyria" reigns supreme.

Right Opened in 2002 "Xcelerator" is located at Buena Park, CA—see p. 159 for more details.

Acknowledgments
Thanks to Mark Franklin for the roller coaster diagrams.
Also thanks in particular for photos, help and information to Alton Towers Resort, Staffordshire, England; Kennywood (®) Park, West Mifflin, PA; and Liseburg Amusement Park, Gothenburg, Sweden. Thanks also to all the other parks and all the many mad thrill ride photographers.

Photo Credits
Alton Towers Resort: 2–3, 182, 191 (Michael Buck).
Getty Images: 6–7, 8 Peter Ptschelinzew, 16–17, 56–57, 71 (T), 126–127, 148–149, 192–193 *The LIFE Picture Collection*, 66–67 Margaret Bourke-White, 98-99 J. Baylor Roberts/National Geographic, 106 Francis Miller, 150 Henry Groskinsky/*The New York Historical Society,* 75 Frank M. Ingalls, 81 Geo. P. Hall & Son, 20 Luis Sinco/*Los Angeles Times*, 65 Joe McNally, 68 Fine Art Images/Heritage Images, 70 Universal History Archive/UIG, 71 (B) SSPL, 76 Chicago History Museum, 93 Smith Collection/Gado, 184 (R) Scott K. Brown/SeaWorld Parks & Entertainment
Library of Congress: pp1, 74 (R), 77, 82 (L), 84 (R), 86 (R)
via Wikimedia Commons/Wikipedia: 72, 73, 78, 79, 81, 82 (L), 91, 92, 96, 131; 5 Naomi, 9, 110–111, 140, 164, 166 Coasterman1234, 37 Fårupsommerland1975, 10 Fastily, 11 Sebastian Hirsch, 18, 34, 95, 122, 133, 147, 198, 203 Martin Lewison, 30 Steven Lek, 19 Pablo Costa Tirado, 21 (B), 202 Freddo, 21 (T) Lar, 22 Peet13, 23 Larry Pieniazek, 24, 59 (L) Elidion, 37 Bgtbbum, 25, 47, 51, 162, 172, 190, 200, 205 Stefan Scheer, 26 Duchess of Bathwick, 27 Kuba Boz anowsk, 28 Jared and Corin, 29, 41 WillMcC, 31, 33, 43, 50, 53, 80, 101 (L), 103, 113, 130, 137, 138, 142 (R), 143, 146, 152, 155, 156, 160, 169, 174 (L), 174 (R), 178, 180, 181, 196, 204 Jeremy Thompson, 32 Cmedinger, 35 kallerna, 36 Chester, 38 Herry Lawford, 39 Sotti, 40 Joeopitz, 42 Craig Lloyd, 44 Arabsalam, 45 Mentalmeltdown, 48 Cmedinger, 49 Aaron Clausen, 50 BiellaLL, 52 BenBowser, 54 (L) Ben Schumin, 54 (R) Oleg Alexandrov, 55 Jerome Dominici, 59 (R) HarshLight, 59 (L) Wikimizuk, 60 Fårupsommerland1975, 69 Koller Auktionen, 70 (inset) Karl_Bodmer, 74 (L), 85 Cedar Fair, L.P., 82 (R) Stevage, 83 Urgeback, 84 (L) Stuart Spivack, 86 Smith, James R., 87 Heyboer Stationery Co., Grand Rapids, Mich., Cedar Fair, L.P., 88 E090, 89 Boston Public Library Tichnor Brothers collection #82569, 90 Visitor7, 94 Blackpool Pleasure Beach, 97 (R) New Zealand Centennial Exhibition, 97 (L) Archives New Zealand, 100 (L) Boston Public Library, Tichnor Brothers Collection, 100 (R) Toronto History, 101 (R) S. Jones, 102 Rollepelle, 104, 142 (L), 163, 201 rollercoasterphilosophy, 105 Robert J. Levy, 107 Alex Proimos, 108 (L) Loadmaster (David R Tribble), 108 (R), 176 SFOTPR, 109 Nick Nolte, 110, 111 (T), 111 (B) Chris Hagerman, 112 Eric Marshall, 114 John Margolies, 115 Alan Light, 116 CillXC, 117 Canobielakepark, 118 Sam Howzit, 119 Bmrbarre, 123, 134, JZ85, 124 cezzie901, 125 Eric Marshall, 128 Shocontinental Evasion Photography, 129 Tim, 132 AmaryllisGardener, 135, 188 Gregory Varnum, 136 (L) Nuclear froggy, 136 (R) Wolfgang Staudt, 139 Gabriel Rinaldi, 141 Christophe Badoux, 144 Parthrb, 145 DAllardyce, 151 Deron Meranda, 153 Alpsdake, 154 Thomas Wagner, 157 Erechtheus, 158 David Fulmer, 159, 165 Dusso Janladde, 161 Mrprogrammer8, 167 Vantey, 168 Pablo Costa Tirado, 170 Michael Gray, 171 Fritz Spitzkohl, 173 Jazon88, 175 Basilico, 177 Alex Brogan, 179 Pitlane02, 184 (L) Jared, 185 Josh Hallett, 186 METRO96, 187 TimvdH96, 189 James Loesch, 194 pixabay, 195 Kotsy, 197 Gerstlauer Amusement Rides GmbH, 199 Christophe Badoux, 206 Rhododendrites, 207 Kikker-8-Baan

Contents

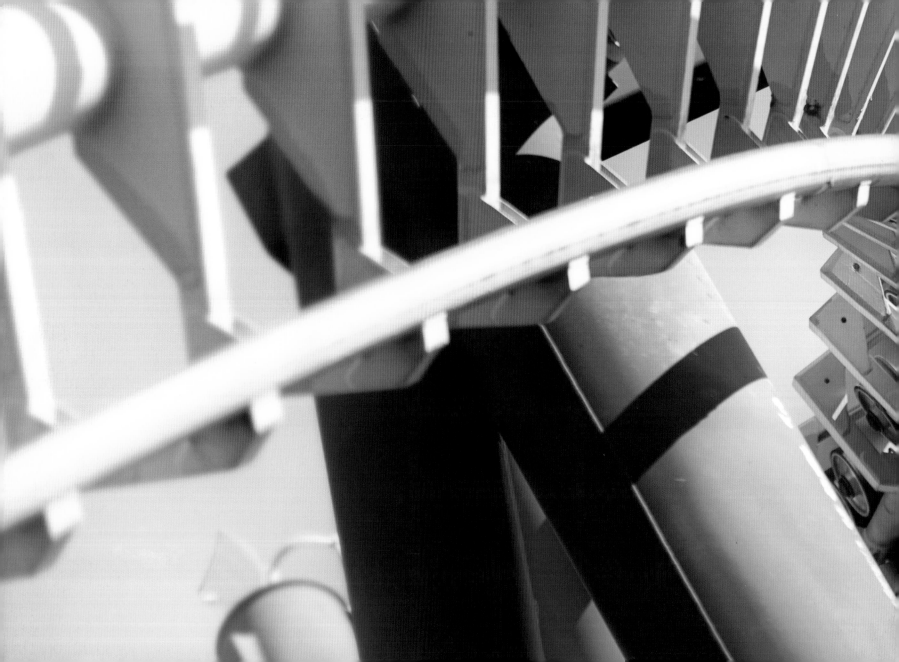

Introduction:
What Makes a Thrill Ride?

Left Thrill rides can be found in all sorts of unexpected places—here the roller coaster "High Roller" (aka "Let it Ride High Roller") can be seen above the main part of the Las Vegas Stratosphere tower shortly before it was dismantled in 2005. It started 909 feet (277 m) above the ground and was definitely not for the faint-hearted!

Right "Raptor" at Cedar Point, Sandusky, Ohio, shows just how extreme the ride can be. See page 133 for details of its terrifying ride.

There is no exact definition of what a thrill ride is, other than that it must be some form of conveyance that thrills its passengers. There are two basic types—active and passive. The former includes such things as being the pilot of a fast jet, or the rider/driver of a sports motorcycle/racing car.

The latter category covers the area that this book is interested in, and covers things like roller coasters, water rides, and drop towers where the thrill is accompanied by the release of copious shots of adrenaline. It also includes, however, more gentle attractions like ferris wheels which excite instead by giving the rider a combination of height and incredible views over the surrounding landscape—altogether more sedate thrills, but thrills nevertheless!

Roller coasters are designed to exploit the fundamental laws of physics. Once they have been brought up to speed by whatever launch system is in use, it is a mix of gravity and inertia that keeps them going. The exception to this, of course, is where the ride's designer has deliberately included one or more lift hills that require artificial assistance to get the train up to the desired height.

It seems that every time a new technology is employed, however, sooner or later it is displaced by a different and better one. This is especially true where catapult launching techniques are used, with examples being things like the introduction of hydraulics, pneumatics, linear induction motors (LIM) and linear synchronous motors (LSM).

Designers have also been pushing the boundaries of how the riders travel—putting them out on wings, hanging them upside down, spinning them around and making them feel like they are flying, are just a few examples.

One of the ways in which the parks make their rides more interesting is by giving them themes and/or by adding various kinds of theatrical trackside scenery. This can include everything from abandoned cars, to disused mining equipment, synthetic landscapes, and so on.

"High Roller"
Las Vegas, Nevada

Status	Removed
Opening date	April 29, 1996
Closing date	December 30, 2005
Type	Helix drop tower
Cost	$900,000
Manufacturer	S&MC
Designer	Premier Rides
Lift/launch system	Tires
Drop	20 ft (6.1 m)
Length	865 ft (264 m)
Speed	30 mph (48 km/h)
Duration	40 sec
Capacity	700 riders per hour

One train of seven cars (originally nine). Riders two x two rows: twenty-eight riders per train

The Driving Forces

Thrill rides come in several forms including roller coasters, drop towers, water rides, and Ferris wheels. Some, of course, are combinations of one or more of the above, however, they all rely on movement of one kind or another.

Ferris wheels sit in a category of their own as they are usually driven by relatively simple electric motors, although the power for these may be from renewable sources, such as solar panels. A good example being the "Pacific Wheel" at the Santa Monica Pier in California.

All of the others rely on gravity to a greater or lesser extent. Most of the simpler water rides such as log flumes simply let the boats go and allow them to be carried downstream to the finish. Drop towers which haul the riders to the top obviously need power to achieve this, but from there they usually just release the carriage, or they may power it to add extra acceleration—and thrills!

Left A view from high on an incline shows how gravity can be exploited to impart movement to a roller coaster. This is "Gold Striker," a wooden ride built by Great Coasters International at California's Great America amusement park.

The very first roller coasters relied entirely on gravity to get them moving and then combined it with inertia to get the cars along the track and down to the finish. Dull rides did not succeed commercially, however, so there was good reason to search for ways to provide increased excitement. Park owners therefore looked for ever more complex ways in which to make their rides more interesting.

Initially, this was done by just adding speed, but then their designers began to push the boundaries of track layouts—this included such things as including loops. Unfortunately, a great number of people were injured in the early days simply because no-one understood where the limits were, or how to engineer the structures to reduce G-forces. A loop that is circular, for instance, will impart shock loadings that can cause permanent physical damage. By adjusting it to what is known in roller coaster circles as a "clothoid form," a loop can be made fun but not dangerous. Properly called an Euler spiral, this shape is essentially a way of transitioning something that is traveling in one direction to another while minimizing the centripetal acceleration (i.e. G-force) it experiences.

Right The Immelmann loop is an important part of the ride on "Griffon," a steel dive coaster at the Busch Gardens, Williamsburg, Virginia. This 180 degree turn sees a rider undergo a half-loop and then a half twist before exiting in the opposite direction.

Track Layouts and Ride Design

There are a number of factors that constrain how a ride can be built—not least of which are the practical ones of budget, terrain, available space, and what rides the park may or may not already have, and so on.

Where the terrain is concerned, there are two things to consider—whether the natural topography lends itself to the task in hand, and whether the underlying geology is suitable for the necessary foundations and numerous structural supports.

At the end of the day, unless the park in question is sited in unbounded wilderness, it is usually of paramount interest to get as much track as is feasible into the smallest possible area. Good layouts try to squeeze in as many elements as possible—hills, turns, loops, drops, and so on, into the tiniest footprint. The more varied and extreme the ride, the greater its appeal to thrill seekers.

Many roller coasters are built with the adjoining landscape in mind to portray and emphasize a particular theme. For example, many of the mine train rides are built across already rocky terrain: this makes sense both financially and aesthetically. Some coasters, however, take this a step further, so that the ride itself is the integral part of an overall story or theme—the "Loch Ness Monster" at Busch Gardens, Williamsburg for example, reflects the mythical beast. Others take cartoon or literary characters like the various Superman and Batman rides as their central theme and storyline. These rides are usually found at the movie studio theme parks run by The Walt Disney Company or Universal Studios.

A different take on this idea is found with the so-called "dark ride," where the coaster undertakes a journey through the inside of a building or some other enclosed space. "Revenge of the Mummy" at Universal Studios, Orlando, and "The Twilight Zone Tower of Terror," at Disney Hollywood Studios, Anaheim, are good examples, the latter also having a drop tower built in for added fear factor, just in case there isn't enough already.

Speed in itself is a popular theme too, with "Formula Rossa" at Ferrari World Abu Dhabi, and "Ring Racer" at the Nürburgring motor racing circuit in Germany, and the NASCAR-themed "Imtimidator" at Carowinds, typifying the genre. They all give the rider a taste of what it's like to experience high velocity thrills, top speeds, acceleration, and big G-forces.

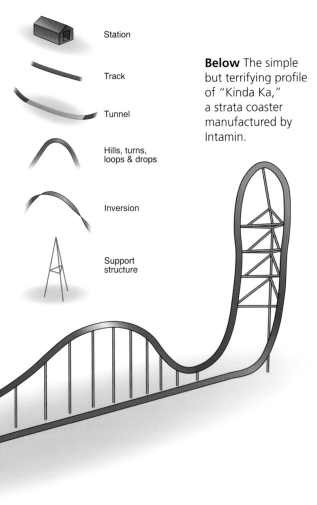

Station

Track

Tunnel

Hills, turns, loops & drops

Inversion

Support structure

Below The simple but terrifying profile of "Kinda Ka," a strata coaster manufactured by Intamin.

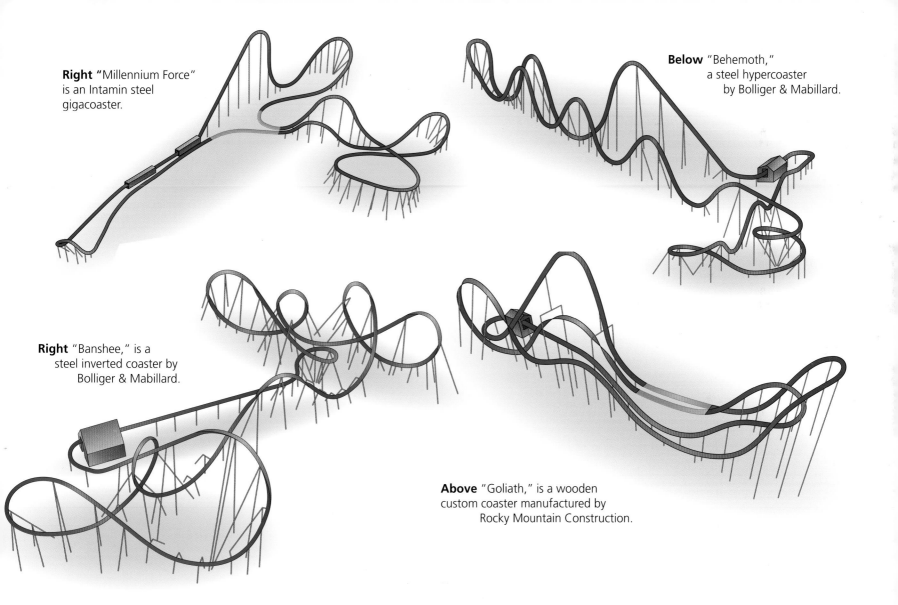

Right "Millennium Force" is an Intamin steel gigacoaster.

Below "Behemoth," a steel hypercoaster by Bolliger & Mabillard.

Right "Banshee," is a steel inverted coaster by Bolliger & Mabillard.

Above "Goliath," is a wooden custom coaster manufactured by Rocky Mountain Construction.

Glossary

Air-Powered Launch: A system that uses pneumatics in the form of compressed air to launch a train.

Airtime: The sensation of being weightless that is caused when a rider experiences negative G-Forces when going over a hump or down a drop.

Block: A safety system used on multitrain rides whereby a section of track is only open to a single train at any given time.

Car: A type of carriage in which the riders are seated—several cars are usually joined together to form a train.

Catapult: When the train is accelerated from rest; this can be achieved with a flywheel, a weight, pneumatics, hydraulics, or electrically.

Chain Lift: A lift hill where the train is hauled to the top using a chain system so that it can be released from the maximum height.

Cobra Roll: A double inversion—so named because it looks a bit like the movement of a striking cobra.

Corkscrew: A twisting inversion that looks like a corkscrew—sometimes called a Barrel Roll.

Crossover: Part of a roller coaster ride where one track goes above or under another length of ttrack.

Dark Ride (aka **Enclosed Ride**): A form of roller coaster where part or all of the ride is inside a structure such as a building; particularly used for themed rides.

Drop Tower: An attraction where riders are taken high above the ground and then dropped either in semi-free fall or in a controlled manner.

Dual Track: A roller coaster that has two different tracks.

Dueling Coaster: A form of roller coaster where two tracks are built close to each other to give the impression of competing interaction between trains.

Element: Part of a thrill ride such as a loop, inversion, tunnel, turn, or a themed section.

Family Coaster: A roller coaster ride that has been designed to provide gentle thrill rides that are particularly suitable for young children.

Flat Ride: Rides that are not categorized as roller coasters or water rides, but may well have similarities.

Floorless Coaster: Roller coasters that have been designed so that the train is above the track but without a floor.

Flying Coaster: Roller coasters that hang beneath the track and reposition the riders so that they are placed in the "Superman" flying stance.

Flying Turns: The original name for bobsled roller coasters.

G-Force: The forces that are imposed as a ride accelerates, decelerates, or travels through an element; measured as fractions of gravity.

Gigacoaster: A coaster that is between 300 feet (91.44 m) and 400 feet (121.92 m) in height off the ground.

Hydraulic Launch: A system that uses hydraulic fluids to launch a train; it is usually used to obtain maximum acceleration.

Hypercoaster: A coaster that is between 200 feet (60.96 m) and 300 feet (91.44 m) in height.

Inversion: A section of a roller coaster track where the rider is turned upside down.

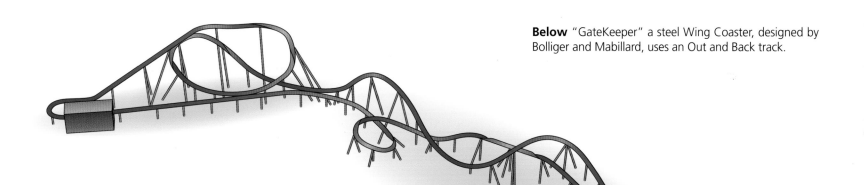

Below "GateKeeper" a steel Wing Coaster, designed by Bolliger and Mabillard, uses an Out and Back track.

Launch: A procedure where a train is accelerated from rest to speed.

Lift Hill: An inclined section of a roller coaster track where a train is pulled up by a cable or chain before being released.

Linear Induction Motor (LIM): Where a series of electromagnets are used to accelerate a train—either at a launch point or out on the track.

Log Flume: A water ride where riders sit in boats that follow (usually) specially constructed rivers that may or may not include rapids.

Linear Synchronous Motor (LSM): A more advanced form of the LIM but with more control over the electromagnets; used to accelerate a train.

Megacoaster: An alternative name for a Hypercoaster.

Racing Coaster: A roller coaster that has two tracks which are the same length and over which the adjacent trains race.

SBNO: Standing But Not Operating—a term that is used to describe a ride that has been taken out of service but not dismantled.

Shuttle Coaster: A roller coaster where the train travels to the end of the track and then back again to the start.

Stratacoaster: A coaster that is over 400 feet (121.92 m) in height.

Suspended Coaster: A roller coaster where the train hangs beneath the track on mounts that allow the cars to pivot (swing) freely from left to right.

Train: The term used to describe two or more thrill ride cars that are connected to each other.

Traveling Coaster: A roller coaster designed to be portable—in other words assembled, used, and disassembled with the minimum of effort.

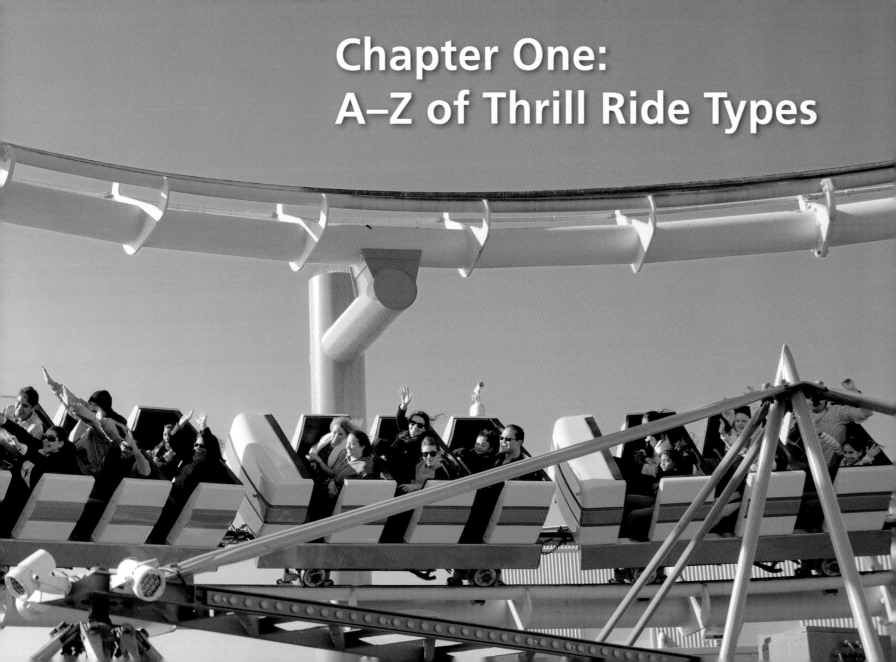

WOODEN THRILL RIDES

Out and Back Coasters

"Tornado"
Adventureland
Altoona, Iowa,

Status	Operating
Opening date	July 4, 1978
Type	Out and back
Manufacturer	Frontier Construction Co.
Designer	William Cobb
Lift/launch system	Chain-lift
Height	93 ft (28 m)
Length	2,850 ft (870 m)
Speed	58 mph (93 km/h)
Duration	2 min

Two trains of four cars. Riders two x three rows: twenty-four riders per train

Out and back coasters are so called because they have a very basic layout—in essence, the train leaves the start point and goes down to the end of the track where it turns around and comes back. The designers make them far more interesting, however, by including all sorts of things such as hills and dips, making them run backwards, and setting them up to race or duel.

Left "Tornado" is a great example of an out and back ride.

Plug and Play Coasters

"El Toro"
Six Flags Great Adventure, Jackson, New Jersey

Status	Operating
Opening date	June 12, 2006
Type	Plug and play, out and back
Cost	$25 million
Manufacturer	Intamin
Designer	Werner Stengel
Model	Wooden Coaster (prefab track)
Lift/launch system	Cable lift hill
Height	181 ft (55 m)
Drop	176 ft (54 m)
Length	4,400 ft (1,300 m)
Speed	70 mph (110km/h)
Duration	1 min 42 sec
Max vertical angle	76 degrees
Capacity	1,500 riders per hour

Two trains with six cars. Riders two x three rows: thirty-six riders per train

A plug and play roller coaster is designed and built so that it comes ready to be assembled on site with a full set of instructions. This massively reduces both the cost and construction time, and allows the manufacturers to refine the design and impose rigorous quality standards.

Above "El Toro" ("The Bull"), an Intamin ride that is located at Six Flags Great Adventure in New Jersey. It was the fastest and steepest wooden coaster when it opened on June 12, 2006.

Racing Coasters

Racing coasters feature two tracks that run alongside each other. The trains race against each other to get to the finish first. A more exciting version is known as the "dueling" coaster, where all manner of elements are introduced to thrill the riders, such as close crossovers and tracks that head towards each other seemingly to collide before sweeping away again.

Only three extant wooden rides incorporate a Moebius loop track layout—one continuous track that doubles back on itself and ends up back at the beginning, but on the other side! These three rides are "Racer" at Kennywood, Pennsylvania, "The Grand National" at Blackpool, UK, and "Serpiente de Fuego" in Chalpultepec Park, Mexico City.

"Colossus"
Six Flags Magic Mountain, Santa Clarita, California

Status	Upgraded to steel
Opening date	June 29, 1978
Closed	August 16, 2014
Type	Racing Moebius loop
Cost	$7 million
Manufacturer	International Amusement Devices
Lift/launch system	Chain lift hill
Height	125 ft (38 m)
Drop	115 ft (35 m)
Length	4,325 ft (1,318 m)
Speed	62 mph (100 km/h)
G-Force	3.2 Gs
Duration	2 min 30 sec

Six trains of six cars. Riders two x two rows: twenty-four riders per train

Left An impressive construction that lives up to its name—"Colossus" at Six Flags Magic Mountain, Santa Clara, was a classic wooden racing ride that was changed several times over its thirty-six year lifetime before it was reconfigured as a steel ride and renamed "Twisted Colossus."

Racing / Moebius Loop Coasters

"Joris en de Draak"
Efteling, The Netherlands

Status	Operating
Opening date	July 1, 2010
Replaced	Pegasus
Type	Racing
Cost	12 million Euros
Manufacturer	Great Coasters International
Model	Racing roller coaster
Lift/launch system	Chain
Height	72 ft (21.9 m)
Drop	72 ft (21.9 m)
Length	2,585 ft (787.9 m)
Speed	47 mph (75.6 km/h)
Inversions	None
Duration	2 min

Four trains of twelve cars. Riders two x one row: twenty-four riders per train

Below Another fine example of a racing track thrill ride is "Joris en de Draak" (in English this translates as "George and the Dragon"), a wooden racing coaster that is located at the Efteling theme park in the Netherlands.

Right "Racer" ready to roll at the platform in Kennywood.

Side Friction Coasters

"Scenic Railway"
Dreamland, Kent, UK

Status	Operating
Opening date	July 3, 1920
Type	Scenic railway
Designer	John Henry Isles
Lift/launch system	Cable (two lifts)
Height	40 ft (12 m)
Drop	40 ft (12 m)
Length	3,000 ft (910 m)
Speed	35 mph (56 km/h)

Three cars per train. Riders two x five rows: twenty eight riders per train

Side-friction coasters are so-called because they feature trains with wheels at the sides and underneath. This primitive system which was pioneered in the late 1800s was later replaced by much more advanced designs.

There are two main kinds of coasters in this category—Scenic Railways and Figure Eight (sometimes also known as Bobsleds). Since Scenic Railways aren't secured to the track, they have a brakeman who controls the speed by slowing the train in the relevant places.

Left The "Scenic Railway" first opened in 1920, and is located at Dreamland, Margate, Kent and is the oldest surviving thrill ride in Britain. It was damaged by fire in April 2008.

Terrain Coasters

"Jack Rabbit"
Kennywood, West Mifflin, Pittsburgh, Pennsylvania

Status	Operating
Opening date	1920
Type	Terrain out and back
Cost	$50,000
Manufacturer	Harry C. Baker
Designer	John A. Miller
Lift/launch system	Chain lift
Height	40 ft (12 m)
Drop	70 ft (21 m)
Length	2,132 ft (650 m)
Speed	45 mph (72 km/h)
Inversions	None
Duration	1 min 15 sec

Three trains of three cars. Riders two x three rows: eighteen riders per train

A terrain coaster is so-named because it is designed to optimize the ups and downs of the land it is sited on. Most tracks are quite close to the ground which gives a better impression of speed—in this situation, a wooden structure is considered to be better than steel for the passengers as it is more flexible and thus gives a softer ride.

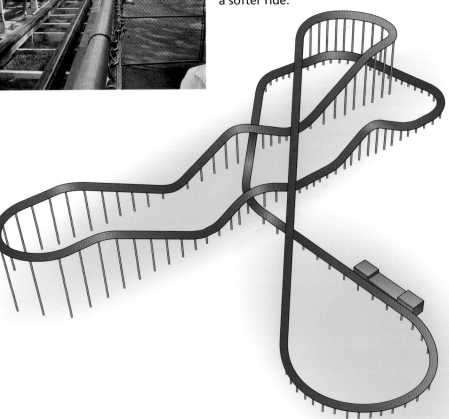

Right "Jack Rabbit" shows the ground-hugging nature of terrain coasters. It first opened in 1921, and is located at Kennywood Park in West Mifflin, near Pittsburgh, Pennsylvania.

Twister Coasters

"Heidi The Ride"
Plopsaland De Panne, Belgium

Status	Operating
Opening date	April 2, 2017
Type	Twister out and back
Cost	7 million euros
Manufacturer	Great Coasters International
Designer	Jeff Pike
Lift/launch system	Chain lift hill
Height	72.2 ft (22 m)
Length	2,056 ft (627 m)
Speed	44 mph (71 km/h)
Duration	1 min 15 sec

Two trains of six cars. Riders two x one row: twelve riders per train

Twister roller coasters are designed to excite through a combination of high speeds and thrilling cornering. One of the advantages of this format is that it allows a thoroughly fulfilling ride to be built on a relatively small footprint—as a result, it is popular with park owners. Some sites have extra elements built in to improve the experience still further, such as unexpected tunnels and fearsome drops.

Below "Heidi The Ride" is a modern, small but thrilling wooden coaster that provides a ride full of airtime and exciting curves.

Wild Mouse Coasters

"Wild Mouse"
Blackpool, UK

Status	Demolished
Opening date	1958
Closing date	2017
Type	Wild mouse
Manufacturer	Pleasure Beach Blackpool
Designer	Frank Wright
Height	50 ft (15 m)
Length	1,266 ft (386 m)
Speed	35 mph (56 km/h)
Inversions	None
Duration	1 min 30 sec
G-force	1.8 Gs

Twelve cars. Riders sit in line: two per car

Wild mouse coasters were once relatively common, however, there are very few still in existence these days. The first to be built was "Devil's Chute," which opened in 1951 at Clarence Pier, Portsmouth, Hampshire, UK.

Right Until the close of the 2017 season, "Wild Mouse" was one of only five Wild Mouse coasters still operating. To its fans dismay, no forewarning of closure was made. Although it first opened in 1958, it was still regarded as an extreme ride.

STEEL THRILL RIDES

Air Coasters

Air coasters use compressed air to power the launch—although they are not as technically elegant as those which use hydraulic systems, they accelerate faster. They can hit enormous G-forces and are an ultimate ride for true thrill ride enthusiasts.

Air thrill rides are defined by the "air time" they achieve giving their passengers a weightless—zero gravity—experience. This is managed when a hurtling train crests a high hill and then drops away down the other side: the momentum of the riders keeps them speeding skywards and momentarily overtakes the Earth's gravitational force, so giving them air time.

Left "Powder Keg: A Blast in the Wilderness" at Silver Dollar City—can reach 100 mph (160 km/h) in just two seconds. "Do Dodonpa" at Fuji-Q Highland in Japan is even faster, reaching 107 mph (172 km/h) in just 1.8 seconds.

"Powder Keg: A Blast in the Wilderness" Silver Dollar City, Missouri

Status	Operating
Opening date	2005
Type	Air
Manufacturer	S&S Worldwide
Designer	Drew Schlie
Lift/launch system	Transfer track; or compressed air launch; or chain lift hill
Height	98 ft (30 m)
Drop	110 ft (34 m)
Length	3,506 ft (1,069 m)
Speed	64 mph (103km/h)
Duration	2 min 53 sec
G-force	3.9 Gs

Three trains of four cars. Riders two x two: sixteen riders per train

Alpine or Mountain Coasters

Alpine coasters—sometimes called mountain coasters, were originally based on alpine slides that used troughs to guide rides that acted like bobsleds on wheels. The coasters—which are gravity driven, took this one stage further by using steel rails with wheels that prevented them from lifting away. They are unlike most roller coasters, however, in that the riders have a degree of control via a braking system.

The rides generally feature a mix of fast banked turns, tunnels, and sudden drops. The tracks can vary from single monorail type systems through to twin parallel tubular steel rails. These allow the coasters to function for most of the year, since they can cope with everything from high temperatures (unlike ice chutes) through to light snow.

Below The alpine ride at Szczesliwice Park, Poland—note the comprehensive safety nets on either side of the rails.

"Gravity Train"
Szczesliwice Park, Warsaw,
Poland

Status	Operating
Type	Alpine
Manufacturer	Wiegand
Length	2,345 ft (715 m)
Speed	22 mph (36 km/h)

Trains of thirty-two cars. Riders two x one: 64 riders per train

Bobsled Coasters

"Alpine Bobsled"
Great Escape, Queensbury, New York

Status	Operating
Opening date	1998
Type	Bobsled
Manufacturer	Intamin
Lift/launch system	Chain lift hill
Height	64 ft (20 m)
Length	1,490 ft (450 m)
Speed	35 mph (56 km/h)
Duration	1 min 40 sec

Six trains of one car. Riders two x four rows: eight riders per train

Left "Alpine Bobsled" was at both Six Flags Great Adventure and Six Flags Great America, before arriving at Great Escape in Queensbury, New York.

Bobsled coasters are so named because they resemble bobsleighs. Unlike most other coasters, with these, the riders sit behind one another in a single line. The experience is aimed at speed through banked corners—to mimic the way bobsled athletes perform, and, in a similar manner, this is achieved entirely through gravity. The first bobsled coaster was patented by John Norman Bartlett, and his first ride was opened in 1929 at the former Lakeside Park, Ohio. This was called "Flying Turns," and was the first of eight such constructions. The designs have come a long way since then.

Boomerang Coasters

"Boomerang" Coaster on site at 55 locations

Status	In production
First manufactured	1984
Manufacturer	Vekoma
Height	116.5 ft (35.51 m)
Length	935 ft (285 m)
Speed	47 mph (76 km/h)
G-Force	5.2
Duration	1 min 48 sec
Inversions	Three

One train of seven cars. Riders two x fourteen rows: twenty-eight riders per train

Right The "Boomerang" at Wild Adventures, Valdosta, Georgia.

There are more examples—over 50—of the boomerang model of coaster, manufactured by Vekoma, than any other in existence. This is partly because they are cheap to install, but also because they don't take up much space, making them suitable for a lot of the smaller parks which couldn't afford one of the larger examples. The ride begins when the train is hauled backwards up a steep incline— once at the top, it is released, whereupon it plummets back down and into what is known as the "Cobra Roll." After that, it goes through a vertical loop and then up another hill. Since there isn't enough momentum to get it to the top, it is mechanically hauled up, before being released to repeat the ride in reverse.

Catapult Coasters

One of the challenges a roller coaster designer faces is just how to get the ride up to speed. Although gravity is effective, it takes time and distance, neither of which provide thrilling passenger experiences. Getting things going in the shortest possible distance is often the goal, and for this an effective launch system is required. There are several methods in use, all of which are based on some kind of catapult. They vary from Zamperla's flywheel-driven launch, to Schwarzkopf's shuttle loop that uses a dropping weight to generate its power.

"Xpress: Platform 13," Walibi, Netherlands

Status	Operating
Opening date	2014
Type	LSM coaster
Manufacturer	Vekoma
Lift/launch system	LSM launch
Height	84.7 ft (25.8 m)
Length	3,267.8 ft (996 m)
Speed	60 mph (96.5 km/h)
Inversions	Three
Duration	1 min 15 sec
G-force	5 Gs

Two trains of six cars. Riders two x two: 24 riders per train

Left The first LSM coaster erected in Europe was an extreme steel ride that was launched as "Superman The Ride" in April 2000. It was renamed "Xpress" in 2005, and then "Xpress: Platform 13" in 2014. It is themed around an abandoned subway station.

Corkscrew Coasters

"Corkscrew"
Michigan's Adventure,
Muskegon County, Michigan

Status	Operating
Opening date	1979
Type	Corkscrew
Manufacturer	Arrow Dynamics
Height	70 ft (21 m)
Speed	45 mph (72 km/h)
Inversions	Two

Six cars per train. Riders two x two rows: twenty-four riders per train

One of the ride experiences that designers really wanted to achieve was a full looping corkscrew coaster to whirl riders around a full 360 degrees. The first successful example was designed by Arrow Development, who produced the "Knott's Berry Farm's Corkscrew" which opened in 1975.

Right "Corkscrew" at Michigan's Adventure, Muskegon County, Michigan, puts its riders through a double corkscrew.

Dive Coasters

Also known as vertical drop coasters, dive machines, Euro-fighters, infinity coasters or el loco coasters. The Dive Coaster was first produced by Bolliger & Mabillard in 2005, when they manufactured and installed the ride "Oblivion" at Alton Towers, Staffordshire, UK. Since then, several other companies have made their own versions.

"Griffon"
Busch Gardens, Williamsburg

Status	Operating
Opening date	May 18, 2007
Type	Dive twister
Cost	$15,600,000
Manufacturer	Bolliger & Mabillard
Lift/launch system	Chain lift
Height	205 ft (62 m)
Drop	205 ft (62 m)
Length	3,108 ft (947 m)
Speed	71 mph (114 km/h)
Inversions	Two
Duration	3 min
G-force	4 Gs

Three trains of three cars. Riders ten x single row: thirty riders per train

Left This is a later model "Griffon," also manufactured by Bolliger & Mabillard, and also called "Griffon" which operates at Busch Gardens Williamsburg. It replaced a ride called "LeMans Raceway."

Floorless Coasters

"SheiKra"
Busch Gardens Tampa, Florida

Status	Operating
Opening date	May 21, 2005
Type	Floorless dive twister
Cost	$13.5 million
Manufacturer	Bolliger & Mabillard
Lift/launch system	Chain lift hill
Height	200 ft (61 m)
Length	3,188 ft (972 m)
Speed	70 mph (110 km/h)
Inversions	One
Duration	2 min 20 sec
G-force	4 Gs

Two trains of three cars. Riders eight across x single row: twenty-four riders per train

Floorless coasters are another form of ride pioneered by Bolliger & Mabillard—their first such installation was called "Kraken" which was sited at SeaWorld Orlando in Florida. Indeed, they are the only company to produce this form of coaster. It uses a series of inversions to create a multilooping experience.

Right "SheiKra" at Busch Gardens, Tampa. When it first opened it took the world records for fastest, tallest, and longest, dive coaster.

Flying Coasters

Also known as flying coaster, prone coaster, lay-down coaster, and Flying Dutchman. However, the flying coaster is exemplified by Vekoma's "Flying Dutchman" model. This lays riders down into a prone position to gives them the feeling that they are flying. The idea has since been taken up by Bolliger & Mabillard, who have developed it further, as well as by Zamperla who make a cheaper version.

"Nighthawk"
Carowinds, Carolinas

Status	Operating
Opening date	March 20, 2004
Replaced	Carolina sternwheeler riverboat
Type	Flying
Manufacturer	Vekoma
Model	Flying Dutchman
Lift/launch system	Chain
Height	115 ft (35 m)
Drop	103 ft (31 m)
Length	2,766 ft (843 m)
Speed	51 mph (82 km/h)
Inversions	5
Duration	1 min 50 sec
Max vertical angle	53 degrees
Capacity	1,000 riders per hour
G-force	4.3 Gs

Two trains of six cars. Riders four x single row: twenty-four riders per train

Left "Nighthawk," was previously known as "Stealth" (2000–2003), then "Borg Assimilator" (2004–2007). It is located at Carowinds, Carolinas.

Fourth-Dimension Coasters

Also known as 4D, zacspin, free spin and ball coasters. The 4D coaster was originally developed by Arrow Dynamics and installed at Six Flags Magic Mountain, however, it proved to have so many mechanical problems that it ruined the company. The first ride was simply called "X"—it cost $36 million, but needed another $10 million spent on it to make it useable; the new version was renamed "X2." Since then, Intamin developed the similar zacspin, and S&S Worldwide the Free Spin, (first ride was Batman: The Ride).

"Kirnu"
Linnanmäki, Finland

Status	Operating
Opening date	April 27, 2007
Type	Fourth dimension
Cost	About 3,000,000
Manufacturer	Intamin
Designer	Werner Stengel
Height	83.4 ft (25.4 m)
Length	465.11 ft (141.77 m)
Speed	37 mph (60 km/h)
Inversions	None
Duration	1 min
G-force	2.6 Gs

Three cars. Riders four x two rows: eight riders per car

Left Manufactured by Intamin and called "Kirnu," (meaning "Churn"), this is a small structure that features a simple track with the passengers traveling on seats that both spin and rotate.

Gigacoasters

When Cedar Fair and Intamin AG created a new ride called "Millennium Force" in May 2000, they wanted a new label to denote the fact that it was the first to exceed 300 feet in height. They settled upon the name "Gigacoaster," and it has since become the accepted term for any ride between 300 and 399 feet high (91.4m–121.6m).

"Leviathan"
Vaughan, Ontario, Canada

Status	Operating
Opening date	May 6, 2012
Type	Gigacoaster out and back
Cost	$28 million
Manufacturer	Bolliger & Mabillard
Designer	Werner Stengel
Lift/launch system	Chain lift hill
Height	306 ft (93 m)
Drop	306 ft (93 m)
Length	5,486 ft (1,672 m)
Speed	92 mph (148 km/h)
Duration	3 min 28 sec
Max vertical angle	80 degrees
G-force	4.5 Gs

Three trains of eight cars. Riders four x single row: thirty-two riders per train

Left "Leviathan" at Canada's Wonderland—was manufactured by Bolliger & Mabillard and runs red, orange, and yellow trains over a cyan track held up by blue supports.

Half Pipe Coasters

"Half Pipe" Six Flags Elitch Gardens, Denver, CO

Status	Operating
Opening date	May 27, 2004
Type	Half pipe
Manufacturer	Intamin
Designer	Werner Stengel
Model	Half Pipe Coaster
Lift/launch system	LIM
Height	98.4 ft (30 m)
Length	229.7 ft (70 m)
Speed	43.5 mph (70 km/h)
Duration	2 min
G-force	4.5Gs

One train of two cars. Riders eight across x one row: sixteen riders per train

Half-pipe coasters are rides where cars run along a U-shaped track—they are hauled up to full height on one side by linear synchronous motors and then released, whereupon they plummet down the incline and, carried by momentum, make it most of the way up the other side. Once there, gravity takes over and they do the same thing in reverse, shuttling back and forth until they eventually come to a stop. Some thrill ride enthusiasts do not consider half-pipe rides to be true roller coasters.

Hydraulic-Launch Coasters

Hydraulic-launch coasters are, as the name would suggest, rides that are brought up to speed through hydraulic means. It was a technology that was developed by Intamin in the early 2000s, and it quickly displayed its suitability for the role by establishing a number of world records for speed and acceleration, as well as height. The first installation was "Xcelerator" at Knott's Berry Farm, California, which opened on June 22, 2002 and provided exceptional performance and thrill.

"Superman Escape"
Warner Bros. Movie World, Gold Coast, Queensland, Australia

Status	Operating
Opening date	December 26, 2005
Type	Hydraulic launch
Cost	A$16 million
Manufacturer	Intamin
Designer	Werner Stengel
Lift/launch system	Hydraulic Launch
Height	130 ft (40 m)
Drop	130 ft (40 m)
Length	2,490 ft (760 m)
Speed	62 mph (100 km/h)
Duration	1 min 40 sec
G-force	4.2 & -1 Gs

Two trains of five cars. Riders two x two rows: twenty riders per train

Left "Superman Escape," is a later version HLC that was even faster than its predecessors. It accelerates from 0 to 62 mph in two seconds!

Hypercoasters

Also known as megacoasters and speed coasters, hypercoasters are rides that stand (or drop) between 200 and 299 feet (61m–91m) distance. The first example was constructed at Cedar Point Ohio, by Arrow Development (which later became Arrow Dynamics); at a dizzying 205 feet (62 m), it broke several new height records. Although it was a milestone in coaster design, other companies soon upped the ante by significantly improving the ride experience, especially where passenger comfort is concerned.

"Shambhala" PortAventura Park, Salou, Spain

Status	Operating
Opening date	May 12, 2012
Manufacturer	Bolliger & Mabillard
Type	Hypercoaster out and back
Lift/launch system	Chain lift hill
Height	249 ft (76 m)
Drop	256 ft (78 m)
Length	5,131 ft (1,564 m)
Speed	83 mph (134 km/h)
Duration	1 min
G-force	3.8 Gs

Three trains of eight cars. Riders two x two rows: thirty-two riders per train

Left "Shambhala: Expedición al Himalaya" at PortAventura Park in Spain, is the tallest coaster in Europe. It is named after the mythical Himalayan kingdom mentioned in ancient Tibetan texts— sometimes also known in the west as Shangri-la.

Inverted Coasters

Also called suspended looping coasters (SLC) and invert coasters, inverted roller coasters are so named because the trains hang underneath the track—they differ from the traditional suspended type in that the seats are affixed directly to the wheel carriage rather than via a swaying bar.

Inverted rides first appeared in the early 1990s when Bolliger & Mabillard created "Batman: The Ride" at Six Flags Great America. The concept immediately proved to be extremely popular with the public, and so, unsurprisingly, it wasn't long before several clones were built and other companies began offering their takes on the idea.

"Black Mamba"
Phantasialand, Brühl, Germany

Status	Operating
Opening date	AMay 24, 2006
Type	Inverted
Cost	11 million Euros for ride + 11 million Euros for themed area
Manufacturer	Bolliger & Mabillard
Lift/launch system	Chain lift
Height	85.3 ft (26 m)
Drop	88.6 ft (27 m)
Speed	49.7 mph (80.0 km/h)
Inversions	Four
G-force	4 Gs

Two trains of eight cars. Riders four x one row: thirty-two riders per train

Left "Black Mamba," runs for two-thirds of the time underground. It features near impacts with walls and also the tightest helix on a Bollinger & Mabillard coaster.

Linear Induction Motor (LIM) Coasters

LIM coasters are so-named because they use linear induction motors to launch the trains. Although the technology had been known about for a long time, it was first used in coaster construction when two rides called "Flight of Fear" were opened in 1996 at Kings Dominion in Virginia, USA and Kings Island in Ohio, USA. Since that time, several variations have been built, including those with reversed seats and dueling versions.

"Backlot Stunt Coaster"

Canada's Wonderland, Kings Dominion, Virginia, and Kings Island, Ohio

Status	Operating
Opening dates	2005/2006
Type	LIM-launched
Manufacturer	Premier Rides
Designer	Werner Stengel
Lift/launch system	LIM launch track
Height	45.2 ft (13.8 m)
Drop	31.2 ft (9.5 m)
Length	1,960 ft (600 m)
Speed	40 mph (64 km/h)
Duration	1 min 4 sec

Three trains of three cars. Riders two x two rows: twelve riders per train

Left "Backlot Stunt Coaster," here at King's Dominion, is found at three parks and is themed to the finale of the 2003 movie "The Italian Job."

Linear Synchronous Motors (LSM) Coasters

Linear synchronous motors have become established as the most popular method of propulsion in launched coasters. This is because they are both simple and powerful, and contain no moving parts that could go wrong.

The first examples were built in 1997—these were "Superman: The Escape" at Six Flags Magic Mountain in California, and the "Tower of Terror" at Dreamworld in Australia.

"Maverick"
Cedar Point, Sandusky, Ohio

Status	Operating
Opening date	May 26, 2007
Type	Blitz
Cost	$21 million
Manufacturer	Intamin
Designer	Werner Stengel
Lift/launch system	Two LSM-launches
Height	105 ft (32 m)
Drop	100 ft (30 m)
Length	4,450 ft (1,360 m)
Speed	70 mph (110 km/h)
Inversions	Two
Duration	2 min 30 sec

Six trains of three cars. Riders two x two rows: twelve riders per train

Left "Maverick," an Intamin ride located at Cedar Point in Sandusky, Ohio. It replaced earlier rides called "White Water Landing" and "Swan Boats."

Looping Coasters

"10 Inversion Roller Coaster" Chimelong Paradise, Guangdong, China

Status	Operating
Opening date	2006
Type	Looping
Manufacturer	Intamin
Designer	Werner Stengel, Ing.-Büro Stengel GmbH
Height	98.4 ft (30 m)
Length	2,788 ft (850 m)
Speed	45 mph (72 km/h)
Inversions	10
Duration	1 min 32 sec

Seven cars per train. Riders two x two rows: twenty-eight riders per train

Also known as loopers, loop-de-loop coasters, or zykloon loopers. The concept of looping coasters is not new—the first attempts to create them back in the late 1800s were commercially unsuccessful as they often injured the riders. This was because the designers did not realize that the only way to make circular loops work was to travel round them faster than was safe.

It was later found that an upside-down pear shape derived from a geometric shape called an Euler Spiral was far better. More popularly known as a "clothoid," this places the maximum inversion at the top, which minimizes the forces imposed on the passengers.

Left "10 Inversion Roller Coaster," is located at Chimelong Paradise, Guangdong, China. It features two inverted cobra rolls, one vertical loop, two corkscrews, and five heartline rolls, and is an exact copy of "Colossus" at Thorpe Park in UK.

Mine Train Coasters

Left "Colorado Adventure," a Vekoma ride at Phantasialand. The first car is the locomotive with two seats, the others have six seats.

Mine train roller coasters are themed to mimic the trains historically used in mining. They usually have a mock locomotive at the front, with cars styled as railroad carriages of various types. There are, however, several different kinds—some use gravity to propel themselves along a track, whereas others have electric motors to provide motion. Most are based on one of three common themes—runaway trains, mine trains, and the Wild West. Although they are derived from the very first scenic railroads, Six Flags Over Texas, installed the first true mine train in 1966. This was called "Run-A-Way Mine Train," and it also broke new ground for a coaster in that it used steel tracks instead of old-fashioned wooden ones.

Multilooping Coasters

"Olympia Looping"

Status	Operating
Opening date	September 17, 1989
Type	Looper
Manufacturer	BHS
Designer	A. Schwarzkopf, Werner Stengel
Lift/launch system	Drive tire lift hill
Height	110 ft (34 m)
Drop	99 ft (30 m)
Length	4,101 ft (1,250 m)
Speed	52 mph (84 km/h)
Inversions	Five
Duration	1 min 45 sec
G-force	5.2 Gs

Several trains of five cars. Riders two x two rows: twenty riders per train

Left "Olympia Looping" is the largest operating transportable roller coaster in the world. In 2016 it even traveled to London.

Also known as multiloopers or megaloopers, multilooping coasters are a well established and hugely popular concept where the rides are based around a series of inversions. The first modern example was "Schwarzkopf's Thriller"—which had four loops and opened to the public in 1986, but was replaced three years later by "Olympia Looping." The largest portable coaster in existence, it has five loops and weighs in at a massive 900 tons. It is usually based in Germany. It made its debut at the 1989 Münich Oktoberfest and has been traveling around the German carnival and fair circuits (and sometimes beyond) ever since.

Spinning Coasters

Left Flagermusen means "The Bat" in Finnish.

Also known as spinners, spinning wild mouse, or twister coasters. Spinning coasters evolved out of Spinning Wild Mouse designs, such as those produced by Reverchon, but these days they display few of the old features. Typically, these spinning coasters have completely different layouts, and accordingly there are many different kinds of seating arrangements for the passengers. Various interpretations of the genre are manufactured by different companies.

Stand-up Coasters

"Shockwave"
Drayton Manor,
Staffordshire, UK

Status	Operating
Type	Stand-up out and back
Manufacturer	Intamin
Designer	Werner Stengel
Model	Stand-up coaster
Lift/launch system	Chain lift hill
Height	120 ft (37 m)
Drop	110 ft (34 m)
Length	1,640 ft (500 m)
Speed	53 mph (85 km/h)
Inversions	Four
Duration	2 min
G-force	4 Gs

Two trains of one car. Riders four x six rows: twenty-four riders per train

Right "Shockwave" is the only stand-up coaster in the world that has a zero gravity roll.

Also known as standing coasters or stand-ups. As the name would suggest, the passengers remain standing throughout the ride on stand-up coasters. The first was produced by TOGO in 1982, and they went on to manufacture a further seven, of which five are still operating. Intamin soon came up with their own interpretation of the concept, with wider cars and more riders, of which "Shockwave" sited in Drayton Manor, UK, is just one example.

Strata Coasters

In the seemingly never-ending pursuit of ever higher rides, it wasn't long before a new name was needed to describe the latest constructions which exceeded 400 feet (122 m). The term arrived at was Strata Coaster with Cedar Point and Intamin once again pushing the boundaries of what had been achieved before.

What they came up with stunned the public—"Top Thrill Dragster" at Cedar Point was some 100 feet higher than any previous ride, and immediately set a series of new records for both height and speed. It was the tallest roller coaster in the world between 2003–2005 when "Kingda Ka" topped it.

Left On launching, "Top Thrill Dragster" accelerates to 120 mph (190 km/h) in 3.8 seconds which shoots it up a 90 degree incline at the same time as twisting 90 degrees before reaching the top. The stomach-turning drop twists through 270 degrees until leveling out and halted by magnetic brakes.

"Top Thrill Dragster" Cedar Point, Sandusky, Ohio

Status	Operating
Opening date	May 4, 2003
Type	Strata drop
Cost	$25 million
Manufacturer	Intamin
Designer	Werner Stengel
Lift/launch system	Hydraulic launch
Height	420 ft (130 m)
Drop	400 ft (120 m)
Length	2,800 ft (850 m)
Speed	120 mph (190 km/h)
Duration	30 sec

Six trains of five cars. Riders two x two rows (except for first car): eighteen riders per train

Suspended Coasters

"Freedom Flyer" Fun Spot America, Orlando, Florida

Status	Operating
Opening date	June 8, 2013
Type	Suspended family inverted twister
Manufacturer	Vekoma
Lift/launch system	Drive tire
Height	64.3 ft (19.6 m)
Length	1,295.9 ft (395 m)
Speed	34.2 mph (55 km/h)
Duration	1 min 3 sec
G-force	2.5 Gs

One train of ten cars. Riders two x single row: twenty riders per train

Right "Freedom Flyer," a Vekoma suspended family coaster at Fun Spot America. Since December 2016 riders can wear a virtual reality (VR) headset to enhance their ride experience.

Suspended coasters feature trains that hang below the track, but unlike Inverted Coasters, these are attached via a pivoted system that allows them to swing from side to side. The ride therefore feels less "attached" to the surrounding supports.

Although this concept has many benefits, the downside is that it cannot be inverted. The first examples were opened in the mid-1970s; however, it wasn't until the early 1980s that permanent installations were built.

Tire Coasters

Tire coasters are rides that are propelled by driven wheels shod with tires. First patented by coaster designer Anton Schwarzkopf in 1980, they are employed to both accelerate the train and to brake it. Some have the wheels positioned horizontally, whereas others use them in a vertical manner.

"The Incredible Hulk" Islands of Adventure, Universal Orlando Resort, Florida

Status	Operating
Opening date	May 28, 1999
Type	Tire
Manufacturer	Bolliger & Mabillard
Designer	Ing.-Büro Stengel GmbH
Lift/launch system	Tire-propelled
Height	110 ft (34 m)
Drop	115 ft (35 m)
Length	3,800 ft (1,200 m)
Speed	67 mph (108 km/h)
Inversions	Seven
Duration	1 min 15 sec
G-force	4 Gs

Multiple trains of eight cars. Riders four x single row: thirty-two riders per train

Left "The Incredible Hulk" is named for the green comic book hero. Riders are accelerated from 0–40 mph (0–64 km/h) in 2.5 seconds into a ride that is not for the faint-hearted!

Water Coasters

"Poseidon"
Europa-Park, Germany

Status	Operating
Opening date	2000
Type	Water coaster
Manufacturer	Mack Rides
Lift/launch system	Chain lift hill x 2
Height	75.5 ft (23 m)
Length	2,743 ft (836 m)
Speed	43 mph (70 km/h)
Duration	2 min
G-force	3 Gs

One car coaster. Riders two x four rows: eight riders per car

Also known as aqua coasters or liquid coasters. One of the very early thrill rides was the "Water Toboggan" at Cedar Point—this opened in 1890, but it took more than a hundred years for a water-based coaster to come along. The first of these was built by E&F Miler Industries in 1996 at Enchanted Forest in Oregon. It was presented rather like a log flume, unlike most of those operating today.

Right "Poseidon" provides an exciting water ride through the world of ancient Greek mythology and a good soaking from the "Aegean Sea."

Wild Mouse Coasters

"Rattlesnake"
Chessington World of Adventures, UK

Status	Operating
Opening date	1998
Type	Wilde Maus Classic
Manufacturer	Maurer Söhne
Designer	Werner Stengel
Lift/launch system:	Chain lift hill
Height	49.25 ft (15.01 m)
Length	1,213 ft (370 m)
Speed	28 mph (45 km/h)
Duration	1 min 10 sec

One car trains. Riders two x two rows: four riders per car

Right "Rattlesnake" at Chessington World of Adventures, is over 1,000 feet long. It is themed as a Mexican mine train in the Wild West era and runs through suitably evocative scenery.

Alternatively called mad mouse rides, wild mouse coasters are designed to thrill through a mix of speed, stomach-churning drops, and high cornering forces. They use small cars—designed to bring mining carts to mind—seating four or fewer riders. The cars travel on tracks laid out to induce the feeling that they are going to go over the edge on the corners—much as in Indiana Jones and the Temple of Doom. Although they went out of fashion in the 1970s and 1980s and almost disappeared, wild mouse rides have become extremely popular these days, with over 250 installations worldwide.

Wing Coasters

"Skyrush"
Hersheypark, Hershey,
Pennsylvania

Status	Operating
Opening date	May 26, 2012
Type	Wing twister
Manufacturer	Intamin
Designer	Werner Stengel
Lift/launch system	Cable
Height	200 ft (61 m)
Drop	212 ft (65 m)
Speed	75 mph (121 km/h)
Duration	1 min
G-force	5 Gs

Two trains of eight cars. Riders four x
single row: thirty-two riders per train

Also called wing riders or free fly coasters, wing coasters differ from conventional thrill rides in that the seats are disposed either side of the track, rather than above or below it. Due to this lack of structure around the passenger, the ride experience is quite unlike anything else provided by other kinds of rides.

The first design to use this seating arrangement was "X" at Six Flags Magic Mountain in California, although it was technically classed as a 4D coaster.

Left "Skyrush" at Hersheypark becomes "Scarerush" for Halloween. The unusual seating sits four abreast with the central two on the track and the outer riders hanging over the side of the track to "ride on the edge." "Skyrush" hits a maximum vertical angle of 85 degrees.

OTHER KINDS OF THRILL RIDES

Drop Towers

Drop Towers are a popular form of thrill ride where the passengers are strapped into seats on a special structure and then dropped from a great height. The first examples were known as "Giant Drop" models, and were located at Carowinds, California's Great America, and Canada's Wonderland. They opened in 1996 and 1997, with the latter two being the fastest dropping at 62 mph (100 km/h), while the one at Carowinds falls at 56 mph (90 km/h). A later model is called "Gyro Drop," which opened in 1999 at Kings Island and 2003 at Kings Dominion.

"Gyro Drop"
Kings Dominion,
Doswell, Virginia

Status	Operating
Type	Drop tower
Opening date	March 22, 2003
Kings Island	
Status	Operating
Type	Drop tower
Opening date	1999
Manufacturer	Intamin

Riders sit individually encircling the tower

Far Left On "Gyro Drop" at Kings Dominion, riders plunge 27 stories (272 ft) at 72 mph. "Gyro Drop" at Kings Island, sits 56 people and rotates when the motor mechanism is functioning (ie not always) as it drops.

Left "California's Great America" has a number of rides, but none as scary as "Drop Tower: Scream Zone." You drop 227ft at 62mph on Intamin's 1996 masterpiece.

Ferris Wheel

"London Eye"
London, United Kingdom

Status	Operating
Opening date	March 9, 2000
Type	Ferris wheel
Cost	£70 million
Designers	Marks Barfield
Height	443 ft (135 m)
Diameter	394 ft (120 m)
Duration	30 min

Thirty-two continuously rotating capsules of up to twenty-five people who can freely walk around inside

Left On a clear day you can see up to 25 miles (40 km) in all directions from the "London Eye" when the observation car is near the top of the orbit. The wheel turns very slowly, with a single revolution taking 30 minutes—so loading and unloading passengers is achieved without it having to stop.

Ferris wheels don't thrill in the same way as roller coasters and drop towers—instead of providing lashings of speed, acceleration, and fear, the ride experience is based on a gentle enjoyment of the scenery from a great height. The epitome of this is found at the "London Eye" from which one can look along the Thames.

Chapter Two: Thrill Ride Records

FASTEST STEEL THRILL RIDES

Rank	Name	Park	Country	Speed	Manufacturer	Record held
1	"Formula Rossa"	Ferrari World	UAE	149 mph (240 km/h)	Intamin	Nov 2010—present
2	"Kingda Ka"	6 Flags Great Adv.	US	128 mph (206 km/h)	Intamin	May 2005—Nov 2010
3	"Top Thrill Dragster"	Cedar Point	US	120 mph (190 km/h)	Intamin	May 2003—May 2005
4	"Do-Dodonpa"	Fuji-Q Highland	Japan	112 mph (180 km/h)	S&S Worldwide	Dec 2001—May 2003
**	"Red Force"	Ferrari Land	Spain	112 mph (180 km/h)	Intamin	N/A
6	"Superman: Escape from Krypton"	Six Flags MM	US	100 mph (161 km/h)	Intamin	Mar 1997—Dec 2001
**	"Tower of Terror II"	Dreamworld	Australia	100 mph (161 km/h)	Intamin	Jan 1997—Dec 2001
8	"Steel Dragon 2000"	Nagashima Spa Land	Japan	95 mph (153 km/h)	D. H. Morgan Man.	N/A
**	"Fury 325"	Carowinds	US	95 mph (153 km/h)	Bolliger & Mabillard	N/A
10	"Millennium Force"	Cedar Point	US	93 mph (150 km/h)	Intamin	N/A

FASTEST WOODEN THRILL RIDES

Rank	Name	Park	Country	Speed	Manufacturer	Record held
1	"Lightning Rod"	Dollywood	US	73 mph (117 km/h)	Rocky Mountain Const.	June 2016—present
2	"Goliath"	Six Flags Great America	US	72 mph (116 km/h)	Rocky Mountain Const.	June 2014—June 2016
3	"Wildfire"	Kolmården Wildlife Park	Sweden	70.2 mph (113.1 km/h)	Rocky Mountain Const.	N/A
4	"El Toro"	Six Flags Great Adventure	US	70 mph (113 km/h)	Intamin	June 2009—June 2014
*	"Colossos"	Heide Park	Germany	68.4 mph (110.1 km/h)	Intamin	N/A
5	"Outlaw Run"	Silver Dollar City	US	68 mph (110 km/h	Rocky Mountain Const.	N/A
6	"The Voyage"	Holiday World & Splashin' Safari	US	67.4 mph (108 km/h)	The Gravity Group	N/A
7	"The Boss"	Six Flags St. Louis	US	66.3 mph (107 km/h)	Custom Coasters Int.	April 2000—May 2000
8	"American Eagle"	Six Flags Great America	US	66 mph (106 km/h)	Intamin	May 1981—April 2000
*	"Mean Streak"	Cedar Point	US	65 mph (105 km/h)	Dinn Coporation	N/A
9	"The Beast"	King Island	US	64.8 mph (104.2 km/h)	Charles Dinn / Al Collins	April 1979—May 1981
10	"T Express"	Everland	South Korea	64.6 mph (104 km/h)	Intamin	N/A

Above A very convincing model of a raptor that is being prepared for duty on "Jurassic Park: The Ride," at Universal Studios Hollywood.

Left The faces on Do-Dodonpa used to be Father, Mother, Sister, and Baby. They have been changed now to Snake, Zebra, Cheetah, and Strawberry. Whatever the name, it is still one of the fastest rides in the world. See page 156 for details.

Thrill ride designers are forever looking for new ways to provide excitement, and combining roller coasters with water provides them with all sort of possibilities—as can be seen here with "Orkanen," a family inverted coaster built by Vekoma, which opened on June 5, 2013 at Fårup Sommerland at Jylland, Denmark.

TALLEST STEEL THRILL RIDES

Rank	Name	Park	Country	Height	Manufacturer	Record held
1	"Kingda Ka"	6 Flags Great Adv.	US	456 ft (139 m)	Intamin	May 2005—Present
2	"Top Thrill Dragster"	Cedar Point	US	420 ft (130 m)	Intamin	May 2003—May 2005
3	"Superman: Escape from Krypton"	Six Flags	US	415 ft (126 m)	Intamin	Mar 1997—May 2003
4	"Tower of Terror II"	Dreamworld	Australia	377 ft (115 m)	Intamin	Jan 1997—Mar 1997
5	"Red Force"	Ferrari Land	Spain	367 ft (112 m)	Intamin	N/A
6	"Fury 325"	Carowinds	US	325 ft (99 m)	Bolliger & Mabillard	N/A
7	"Steel Dragon 2000"	Nagashima Spa Land	Japan	318 ft (97 m)	D. H. Morgan	N/A
8	"Millennium Force"	Cedar Point	US	310 ft (94 m)	Intamin	N/A
9	"Leviathan"	Canada's Wonderland	Canada	306 ft (93 m)	Bolliger & Mabillard	N/A
10	"Intimidator 305"	Kings Dominion	US	305 ft (93 m)	Intamin	N/A

TALLEST WOODEN THRILL RIDES

Rank	Name	Park	Country	Height	Manufacturer	Record held
1	"Colossos"	Heide Park	Germany	197 ft (60.m)	Intamin	June 2009—present
2	"Wildfire"	Kolmården Wildlife Park	Sweden	187 ft (57 m)	Rocky Mountain Const.	N/A
3	"T Express"	Everland	South Korea	184 ft (56 m)	Intamin	N/A
4	"El Toro"	Six Flags Great Adventure	US	181 ft (55 m)	Inatmin	N/A
5	"Goliath"	Six Flags Great America	US	165 ft (50.2 m)	Rocky Mountain Const.	N/A
6	"The Voyage"	Holiday World & Splash-in' Safari	US	163 ft (49.6 m)	The Gravity Group	N/A
*	"Mean Streak"	Cedar Point	US	161 ft (49 m)	Dinn Corp.	May 1991—March 1992
7	"White Cyclone"	Nagashima Spa Land	Japan	139 ft (42 m)	Intamin	N/A
8	"Hades 360"	Mt. Olympus W&T Park	US	136 ft (41 m)	The Gravity Group	N/A
9	"Wodan Timbur Coaster"	Europa-Park	Germany	131.3 ft (40 m)	Great Coasters Int.	N/A
10	"The Boss"	Six Flags St. Louis	US	122 ft (37 m)	Custom Coasters Int.	N/A
**	"Shivering Timbers"	Michigan's Adventure	US	122 ft (37 m)	Custom Coasters Int.	N/A

LONGEST STEEL THRILL RIDE DROPS

Rank	Name	Park	Country	Drop length	Manufacturer	Record held
1	"Kingda Ka"	Six Flags Great Adventure	US	418 ft (127 m)	Intamin	May 2005—present
2	"Top Thrill Dragster"	Cedar Point	US	400 ft (120 m)	Intamin	May 2003—May 2005
3	"Superman: Escape from Krypton"	Six Flags	US	328 ft (100 m)	Intamin	May 1997—May 2003
4	"Tower of Terror II"	Dreamworld	Australia	328 ft (100 m)	Intamin	Jan 1997—May 2003
5	"Fury 325"	Carowinds	US	320 ft (98 m)	Bolliger & Mabillard	N/A
6	"Steel Dragon 2000"	Nagashima Spa Land	Japan	307 ft (94 m)	D. H. Morgan	N/A
7	"Leviathan"	Canada's Wonderland	Canada	306 ft (93 m)	Bolliger & Mabillard	N/A
8	"Intimidator 305"	Kings Dominion	US	300 ft (91 m)	Intamin	N/A
9	"Millennium Force"	Cedar Point	US	300 ft (91 m)	Intamin	N/A
**	"Unknown"	Energylandia	Poland	265.8 ft (81 m)	Intamin	N/A
10	"Shambhala: Expedición al Himalaya"	PortAventura	Spain	256 ft (78 m)	Bolliger & Mabillard	N/A
**	"Coaster Through the Clouds"	Nanchang Wanada Park	China	256 ft (78 m)	Intamin	N/A

LONGEST WOODEN THRILL RIDE DROPS

Rank	Name	Park	Country	Drop length	Manufacturer	Record held
1	"Goliath"	Six Flags Great America	US	180 ft (55 m)	Rocky Mountain Const.	June 2014—present
2	"El Toro"	Six Flags Great Adventure	US	176 ft (54 m)	Intamin	June 2009—June 2014
3	"Lightning Rod"	Dollywood	US	165 ft (50 m)	Rocky Mountain Const.	N/A
4	"Outlaw Run"	Silver Dollar City	US	162 ft (49 m)	Rocky Mountain Const.	N/A
5	"Wildfire"	Kolmården Wildlife Park	Sweden	161 ft (49 m)	Rocky Mountain Const.	N/A
6	"Colossos"	Heide Park	Germany	159 ft (48 m)	Intamin	N/A
*	"Mean Streak"	Cedar Park	US	155 ft (47 m)	Dinn Corporation	May 1991—May 2000
7	"The Voyage"	Holiday World & Splashin' Safari	US	154 ft (47 m)	The Gravity Group	N/A
8	"T Express"	Everland	South Korea	151 ft (46 m)	Intamin	N/A
9	"The Boss"	Six Flags St. Louis	US	150 ft (46 m)	Custom Coasters Int.	N/A
10	"American Eagle"	Six Flags Great America	US	147 ft (45 m)	Intamin	April 1981—May 1991
11	"The Beast"	Kings Island	US	141 ft (43 m)	Charles Dinn / Al Collins	April 1979—May 1981

LONGEST STEEL THRILL RIDES

Rank	Name	Park	Country	Length	Manufacturer	Record held
1	"Steel Dragon 2000"	Nagashima Spa Land	Japan	8,133 ft (2,479 m)	D. H. Morgan Man.	Aug 2000—present
2	"The Ultimate"	Lightwater Valley	UK	7,442 ft (2,268 m)	British Rail	Jul 1991—Aug 2000
3	"Fujiyama"	Fuji-Q Highland	Japan	6,709 ft (2,045 m)	TOGO	N/A
4	"Fury 325"	Carowinds	US	6,602 ft (2,012 m)	Bolliger & Mabillard	N/A
5	"Millennium Force"	Cedar Point	US	6,595 ft (2,010 m)	Intamin	N/A
6	"Formula Rossa"	Ferrari World	UAE	6,562 ft (2,000 m)	Intamin	N/A
7	"California Screamin'"	Disney California Adventure	US	6,072 ft (1,851 m)	Intamin	N/A
*	"Vertigorama"	Parque de la Ciudad	Argentina	5,958 ft (1,816 m)	Intamin	N/A
8	"Desperado"	Buffalo Bill's	US	5,843 ft (1,781 m)	Arrow Dynamics	N/A
9	"Mamba"	Worlds of Fun	US	5,600 ft (1,700 m)	D. H. Morgan Man.	N/A
10	"Steel Force"	Dorney Park & Wildwater Kingdom	US	5,600 ft (1,700 m)	D. H. Morgan Man.	N/A

LONGEST WOODEN THRILL RIDES

Rank	Name	Park	Country	Length	Manufacturer	Record held
1	"The Beast"	Kings Island	US	7,359 ft (2,243 m)	Charles Dinn / Al Collins	April 1979—present
2	"The Voyage"	Kolmården Wildlife Park	US	6,442 ft (1,964 m)	The Gravity Group	N/A
3	"White Cyclone"	Everland	Japan	5,577 ft (1,700 m)	Intamin	N/A
4	"T Express"	Six Flags Great Adventure	South Korea	5,383.8 ft (1,641 m)	Inatmin	N/A
5	"Shivering Timbers"	Six Flags Great America	US	5,383.8 ft (1,641 m)	Custom Coasters Inc.	N/A
6	"Jupiter"	Holiday World & Splashin' Safari	Japan	5,249 ft (1,600 m)	Intamin	N/A
7	"Python in Bamboo Forest"	Cedar Point	China	5,111 ft (1,558 m)	Great Coasters Int.	N/A
8	"The Boss"	Nagashima Spa Land	US	5,051 ft (1,540 m)	Custom Coasters Int.	N/A
9	"Wood Coaster"	Mt. Olympus W&T Park	China	4,817 ft (1,468 m)	Great Coasters Int.	N/A
10	"Hades 360"	Europa-Park	US	4,746 ft (1,446 m)	The Gravity Group	N/A

MOST INVERSIONS ON A STEEL THRILL RIDE

Rank	Name	Park	Country	Inversions	Manufacturer	Record held
1	"The Smiler"	Alton Towers	UK	14	Gerstlauer	May 2013—present
2	"10 Inversion Roller Coaster"	Chime-Long Paradise	China	10	Intamin	Feb 2006—May 2013
	"Altair"	Cinecittà World	Italy	10	Intamin	N/A
	"Colossus"	Thorpe Park	UK	10	Intamin	March 2002—May 2013
	"Crazy Coaster"	Locajoy Holiday	China	10	Intamin	N/A
	** unknown	Hopi Hari	Brazil	10	Intamin	N/A
	** unknown	Movie Animation Park Studios	Malaysia	10	Intamin	N/A
	** unknown	Wonder Island	Russia	10	Intamin	N/A
	** unknown	Ankapark	Turkey	10	Intamin	N/A
6	"Avalaancha"	Xetulul	Guatemala	8	Intamin	N/A
	"Dragon Khan"	PortAventura Park	Spain	8	Bolliger & Mabillard	May 1995—March 2002
	"Flight of the Phoenix"	Harborland	China	8	Intamin	N/A
	** unknown	Mirabilandia	Brazil	8	Intamin	N/A

MOST INVERSIONS ON A WOODEN THRILL RIDE

Rank	Name	Park	Country	Inversions	Manufacturer	Record held
1	"The Joker"	Six Flags Discovery Kingdom	US	3	Rocky Mountain Const.	May 2016—present
	"Medusa Steel Coaster"	Six Flags Mexico	Mexico	3	Rocky Mountain Const.	June 2014—present
	"Outlaw Run"	Silver Dollar City	US	3	Rocky Mountain Const.	March 2013—present
	"Wicked Cyclone"	Six Flags New England	US	3	Rocky Mountain Const.	May 2015—present
	"Wildfire"	Kolmården	US	3	Rocky Mountain Const.	June 2016—present
2	"Goliath"	Six Flags Great America	US	2	Rocky Mountain Const.	N/A
	"Storm Chaser"	Kentucky Kingdom	US	2	Rocky Mountain Const.	N/A
	"Twisted Colossus"	Mt. Olympus Water & Theme Park	US	2	Rocky Mountain Const.	N/A
3	"Hades 360"	Kentucky Kingdom	US	1	The Gravity Group	N/A
	"Iron Rattler"	Six Flags Magic Mountain	US	1	Rocky Mountain Const.	N/A
	"Jungle Trailblazer"	Oriental Heritage, Ningbo	China	1	The Gravity Group	N/A
	"Jungle Trailblazer"	Oriental Heritage, Jiujiang	China	1	The Gravity Group	N/A
	"Jungle Trailblazer"	Oriental Heritage, Cixi	China	1	The Gravity Group	N/A
	"Mine Blower"	Fun Spot America: Kissimmee	US	1	The Gravity Group	N/A

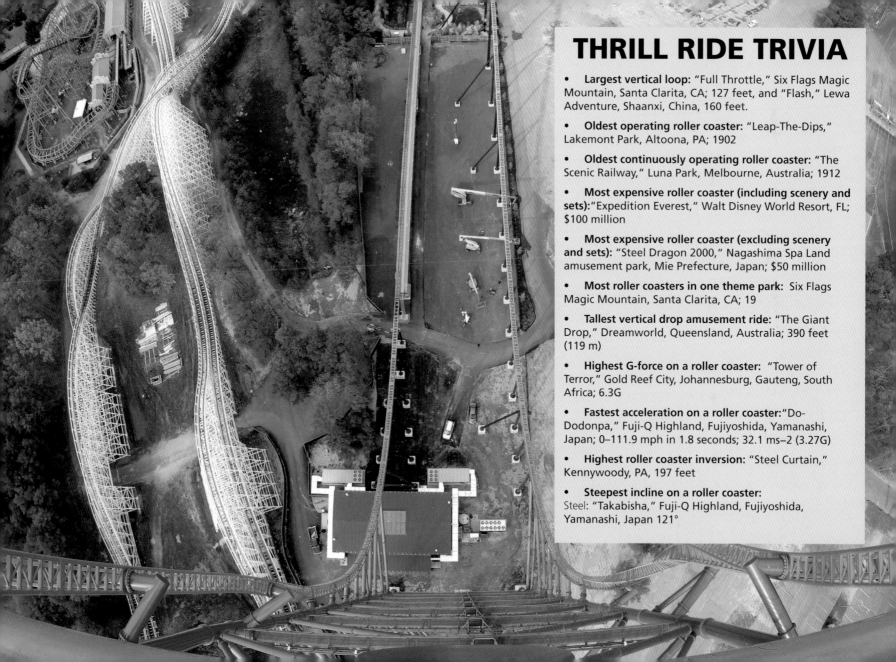

THRILL RIDE TRIVIA

- **Largest vertical loop:** "Full Throttle," Six Flags Magic Mountain, Santa Clarita, CA; 127 feet, and "Flash," Lewa Adventure, Shaanxi, China, 160 feet.

- **Oldest operating roller coaster:** "Leap-The-Dips," Lakemont Park, Altoona, PA; 1902

- **Oldest continuously operating roller coaster:** "The Scenic Railway," Luna Park, Melbourne, Australia; 1912

- **Most expensive roller coaster (including scenery and sets):** "Expedition Everest," Walt Disney World Resort, FL; $100 million

- **Most expensive roller coaster (excluding scenery and sets):** "Steel Dragon 2000," Nagashima Spa Land amusement park, Mie Prefecture, Japan; $50 million

- **Most roller coasters in one theme park:** Six Flags Magic Mountain, Santa Clarita, CA; 19

- **Tallest vertical drop amusement ride:** "The Giant Drop," Dreamworld, Queensland, Australia; 390 feet (119 m)

- **Highest G-force on a roller coaster:** "Tower of Terror," Gold Reef City, Johannesburg, Gauteng, South Africa; 6.3G

- **Fastest acceleration on a roller coaster:** "Do-Dodonpa," Fuji-Q Highland, Fujiyoshida, Yamanashi, Japan; 0–111.9 mph in 1.8 seconds; 32.1 ms−2 (3.27G)

- **Highest roller coaster inversion:** "Steel Curtain," Kennywoody, PA, 197 feet

- **Steepest incline on a roller coaster:**
Steel: "Takabisha," Fuji-Q Highland, Fujiyoshida, Yamanashi, Japan 121°

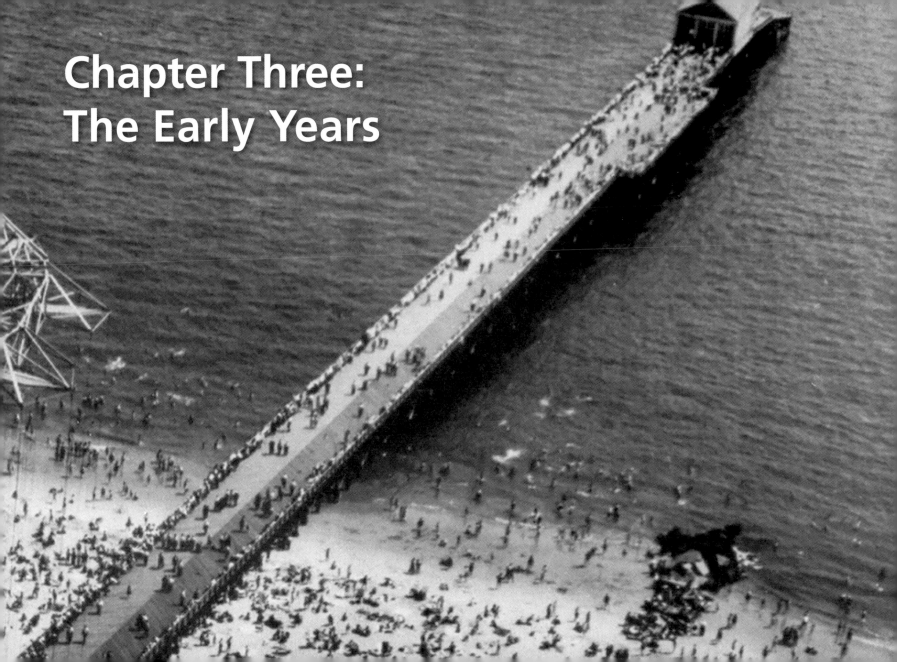

Chapter Three:
The Early Years

THE EARLY YEARS—1899

The lineage of the roller coaster is surprisingly old possibly going as far back as 15th-century Russia, when people bored with the seemingly endless winters built rudimentary rides with wooden sleds and sent them down ice-covered runs in much the same way as modern bobsleds are used.

As time went on, they gradually made the runs more elaborate, and by 1784, there was a ride in St. Petersburg using gravity-powered carriages that ran in grooves cut into the ice.

Early drawings show that some of the rides were constructed from large wooden towers with steps on one side and a u-shaped ice slide on the other. People would climb up the steps, get into a carriage, and then plummet down the slide, with the other end of the slope rising again in much the same manner as a modern half-pipe coaster.

Previous Page Coney Island beach and the parachute drop tower, the framework of which was left in situ after operations ceased around 1964. It was built for the New York World's Fair of 1938.

Below Painting by Benjamin Paterssen of Catherine the Great, Empress of Russia, visiting the ice mountain in St. Petersburg, 1788.

1817: Russian Mountains, Paris, France

The popularity of the Russian ice slides was noted by someone with a nose for business, and a ride called "Les Montagnes Russes" (The Russian Mountains) was built in Paris in 1804. Since creating ice slides was far harder in the temperate climate of France, the constructors fitted small wheels to the carriages instead of skis. This was yet another crucial step in the evolution of the modern roller coaster.

Although these early rides were very basic and injuries commonplace, some clever marketing exploited this, attracting even more customers. Before long many design improvements were made, culminating in the opening in Paris in 1817 of "Les Montagnes Russes de Belleville" (The Belleville Mountains) and the "Promenades Aériennes" (the Aerial Walks). These featured many elements that we would recognize today— such as continuous tracks, more advanced wheels, and cables to hoist the carriages to the top of the slope.

Right Concrete details about early rides are few and far between and often rely on illustrations such as those on these pages from which some details can be inferred. What we can tell, though, is that they were popular attractions.

PROMENADES AERIENNES,

Jardin Baujon.

1827: Mauch Chunk Switchback Gravity Railroad, PA

The Mauch Chunk Switchback Gravity Railroad was originally built in 1827 by the Lehigh Coal & Navigation Company to transport coal to a wharf on the Lehigh Canal in Mauch Chunk. It was 8.7-miles (14.0 km) long, and powered entirely by gravity, with only a single person on board to operate the brakes. Within 20 or so years a sideline business began when they started selling rides down the hill for 50 cents a time—by then it had become known as the "Gravity Road." In 1873 the railway began to use the Hauto Tunnel instead, but the fare-paying customers still wanted the ride, so it reopened in 1873, carrying as many as 35,000 passaengers a year.

The success of the concept provided some of the inspiration for LaMarcus Adna Thompson who later opened a gravity ride at Coney Island in 1884.

Right Bird's Eye view of Mauch Chunk, Pennsylvania, with the Lehigh Canal, the railroad, and mountains in the distance.

Inset Painting dated 1832 by Karl Bodmer shows the terminus end of the Mauch Chunk & Summit Hill Railroad together with the coal chutes.

1846: "Centrifugal Railway," Le Havre, France

In the mid-1800s a number of looping roller coasters were built in various locations around England and France. Generally referred to as centrifugal railways, they featured a short length of track with one hill and a single loop. The rides started at one end and finished at the other—in other words, they did not make a circuit of any kind. One example, known as "The Grand Centrifugal Railway" was built by a company called Dean & Esplin. Although the promotional material claimed that the loops were 80 feet (24 m) in circumference (and thus about 25 feet [7.6 m] high), it was a time when reckless exaggeration was a common marketing feature. The riders were transported in primitive sledges.

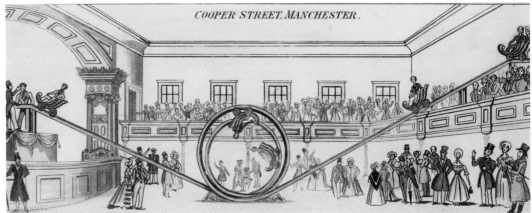

Above Right Centrifugal railway created by the Parisian engineer M. Clavières in Le Havre, France, 1846.

Below Right Dean & Esplin's Grand Centrifugal Railway, Cooper Street Manchester, in the 1850s. It consisted of "two circles 80 feet in circumference" and the participants sat in sledges for the ride, as depicted here.

1878: Knudsen's Inclined-Plane Railway

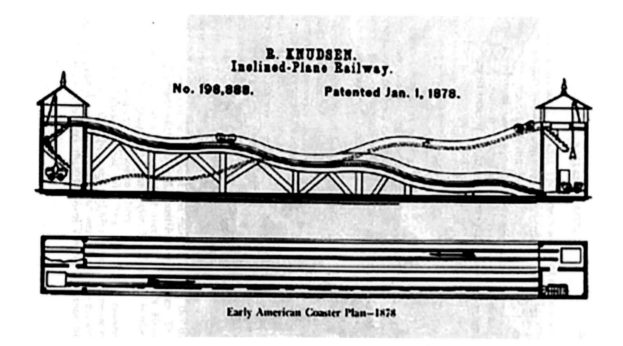

R. KNUDSEN.
Inclined-Plane Railway.

No. 198,888.   Patented Jan. 1, 1878.

Early American Coaster Plan—1878

The evolution of the thrill ride moved a step forwards when the first patent for a gravity-powered roller coaster was obtained by Richard Knudsen in 1878. It was labeled as an "Inclined Plane Railway," but although the idea was good, he never managed to actually open it. Knudsen later added improvements to the patent in 1885.

A year earlier, the Switchback Railway opened at Coney Island in Brooklyn, New York—it proved to be an enormous success commercially, and it inspired many other people to construct their own versions. This was especially true in the UK after Wild Bill Cody put on an American Exhibition at Earl's Court in London. This featured a Switchback Railway and Toboggan Slides which proved to be extremely popular. As a result, switchback railways became an overnight craze with all manner of rides—such as the Hart & Ripley "Patent Safety Switchback" design, being opened in many minor towns and cities across the country.

1885: Thompson's Gravity Switchback Railway

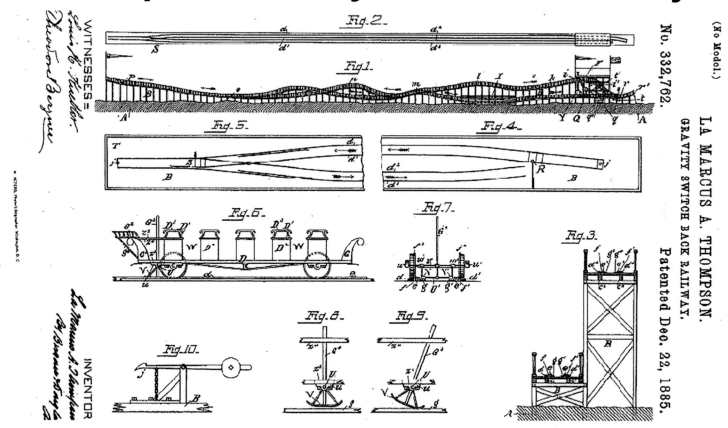

LaMarcus A. Thompson, of Philadelphia, PA, is often credited as inventing the roller coaster. It is certainly true that he submitted a detailed patent application for a Gravity Switch-Back Railway to the United States Patent Office, and it was granted as Patent No.332,762 on December 22, 1885. In essence, it showed how a passenger car would travel out of a pavilion and down an inclined plane via a series of rises and falls, through a tunnel and finally finish in another pavilion. It specified "automatic and sliding switches," sections of the rails, the carriage together with its braking system, and so on. The layout was of a double track nature with the express intention of the ride providing a "source or means of pleasure and amusement."

1890: "Water Toboggan," Cedar Point, NY

The fashion for going on amusement rides in the late 1800s brought great commercial success to many operators. As a result, it inspired the construction of many different kinds of new attractions. Cedar Point, for example, were particularly keen to exploit the popularity of their beach area. The bath houses there—from which people could bathe, rather than swim—were sited near to dance floors and beer gardens, but although they were well attended, they lacked a major draw. This led to the opening of what the owners called "The Water Toboggan" in 1890 and while it certainly drew the crowds in to start with, it wasn't long before more exciting rides were built nearby and it was finally closed sometime early in the 20th century.

Above "The Water Toboggon" was a large structure made from wooden trestles with a long slide on top that reached out into Lake Erie. Customers would climb up a series of steps and then launch themselves down the slide and into the water below.

Right Everyone likes water toboggans—this is from "Shoot-the-Chutes" an 1895 ride on Coney Island.

1884: Switchback Railway, Coney Island, NY

The first roller coaster to be opened in the United States was designed by LaMarcus Adna Thompson in 1881, and opened in 1884. From the similarities in concept, it would seem that his idea was at least partly based on the Mauch Chunk Railway. His principle, however, took the riders from a tower and down a track via a series of rises and dips to a corresponding tower at the other end. Once there, the car would return down a second track so that the passengers would end up back where they started. The ride is thought to have closed in 1907—but it may have been after only a couple of seasons—as the result of newer and better attractions drawing the crowds away.

Status	Removed
Opening date	June 16, 1884
Closing date	c. 1907
Type	Wooden gravity-pulled
Manufacturer	LaMarcus Adna Thompson
Designer	LaMarcus Adna Thompson
Model	Lift-packed
Lift/launch system	Gravity
Height	50 ft (15 m)
Drop	43 ft (13 m)
Length	600 ft (180 m)
Speed	6 mph (9.7 km/h)
Duration	1 min
G-force	2.9 Gs

Left The gentle 30-degree slide of the "Switchback Railway" could accommodate an astonishing 1,600 riders an hour.

1893: Columbian Exposition Ferris Wheel, Chicago, IL

Prince Albert, consort of British Queen Victoria, had the idea for a world's fair—probably prompted by the French Industrial Exposition held in Paris in 1844. The success of the Great Exhibition of 1851 spawned an era of great fairs showing off the wares of the Industrial Revolution. Chicago's was the sixth major fair, and it coincided nicely with the 400th anniversary celebration of Christopher Columbus's arrival in the New World in 1492—which accounts for its name. The World's Columbian Exposition was opened in Chicago in 1893, only 20 years after the city had been devastated by fire.

The fair acted as a vast social and cultural showcase for all the best and newest productions and ideas—for everything from the arts to industry. Among the exhibits were many different fairground rides, including the original Ferris Wheel.

Over 250 feet high, it revolved on a 71-ton, 45-foot axle that had, at the time, the world's largest hollow forging. It was so successful that it was reused after the fair, first in Chicago and then in 1904 for the world's fair held in St. Louis.

Right The biggest attraction at the exposition was the enormous Ferris Wheel constructed by George Washington Gale Ferris Jr. It was 264 feet (80m) high with 36 cars, that each had the capacity to carry 60 passengers. It proved a popular attraction.

1897: "Flip Flap Railroad," Coney Island, NY

Sea Lion Park, at Coney Island—which was established in 1895 by a famous celebrity named Captain Paul Boyton—was the first enclosed amusement park in the United States. Rather than simply buying tickets for rides they wanted to experience, customers paid an entrance fee instead. It wasn't a particularly big venue—only 16 acres, however, it set the scene for the future.

There were many and various attractions, including a ride based on an old water mill, the "Shoot-the-Chutes" water toboggan where customers traveled up an elevator whereupon they climbed into a lightweight boat. This then slid down a slide, up a small ramp before splashing heavily into the lagoon below. The craft was then returned to land for the next consignment of passengers to board. (See page 74 for photo of the "toboggan.")

The 25-foot circumference "Flip Flap Railway" was developed by Lina Beecher (1841–1915), a New Yorker, and was very similar to the European centrifugal railway (see page 71). As with the European predecessors, the huge problem associated with this sort of attraction was the frequency of whiplash injuries caused to the riders. In an age where health and safety issues were less than carefully monitored, the railway is said to have led to 12G forces—one of the problems being its circular rather than elliptical construction.

Beecher went on to modify his design to a more elliptical shape, but his "Loop the Loop" in Columbus, Ohio, was also a failure.

Below Panoramic view of the park with its unique "Flip Flap Railroad." In 1903, Boyton sold up and the attraction was replaced by Luna Park.

1900–1919: BEGINNING OF THE THRILL RIDE ERA

As the nineteenth century ended, the amusement industry was dominated by scenic railroads and fairground attractions. Roller coasters were, however, becoming ever more popular, mostly because their designers had learned a lot of important lessons regarding things like track layouts and rider enjoyment.

Over the next two decades several major theme parks either expanded or opened up anew, and several famous rides were built. Examples include "Loop-the-Loop" at Luna Park, Coney Island and "Leap-The-Dips" at Lakemont Park, Pennsylvania.

Left Chutes Park, Los Angeles photographed around 1906. It shows a tall water slide with a mechanical passenger lift beside it. The affair must have been quite an attraction as there are lots of bench seats arranged around the pool, suggesting big crowds. On the other side of the slide are the tracks of a roller coaster which has signs that read "Tickets 10¢, children 5¢" and "Danger, don't stand up."

1901: "Loop-the-Loop," Coney Island, NY

Luna Park was an amusement park that opened in Coney Island, Brooklyn, New York City in 1903. It was owned by Frederic Thompson and Elmer "Skip" Dundy, and based over the site of Sea Lion Park which they'd taken over from Captain Paul Boyton at the end of 1902.

They did, however, extend it significantly, adding eight acres to bring it up to a total of 22 acres. The park operated through 1944, when it was largely destroyed by fire. It reopened briefly after repairs were carried out, but a second fire did enough damage to force it to close completely in 1946.

"Loop-the-Loop" was located at Coney Island from 1901 to 1910, built in part to improve on the ride experience of the very similar "Flip Flap Railroad." The new version, which featured two tracks, was designed by Edward Green and built by Edwin Prescott. The G-forces were reduced by making the loop more elliptical. Although this was a big step forward from the previous model, it was still uncomfortable to ride, and was not a commercial success.

LOOP THE LOOP, CONEY ISLAND, N.Y.

Right "Loop-the-Loop" was named after the circular loop which imposed vicious loads on its riders—and because of this, it gained a well-earned reputation for causing very sore necks.

1902: "Leap-the-Dips," Altoona, PA

Status	Operating/Restored
Opening date	1902
Type	Wooden side-friction figure of eight
Manufacturer	Federal Construction Company
Designer	Edward Joy Morris
Height	41 ft (12 m)
Drop	9 ft (2.7 m)
Length	1,452 ft (443 m)
Speed	10 mph (16 km/h)
Duration	1 min

One car. Riders two x two rows: four riders a car

"Leap-The-Dips" was built in 1902 at Lakemont Park in Altoona, and is the oldest extant roller coaster in the world. It operated until 1985 when it was withdrawn from service due to a lack of maintenance. It languished unused until 1997, when restoration efforts began. These were completed in 1999, when it was reopened. Lakemont Park started life as a trolley park, became an amusement park in 1899, went through a two-year spell when it was dubbed Boyertown USA, and is currently closed for refurbishment, due to open in 2019.

Right "Leap-The Dips" is probably the last figure-eight, side-friction coaster in existence.

1904: Dreamland Park, Coney Island, NY

Dreamland was opened in 1904 by William H. Reynolds as an amusement park at Coney Island, Brooklyn, New York City. Although it was the most opulent of the three parks on the island, it didn't last very long, being destroyed by fire in 1911. The founder's intention was to go upmarket, with far more elegant buildings and a more genteel atmosphere throughout than its direct rival, Luna Park. The central tower, for example, was bigger and had one million light bulbs highlighting its shape and size. Along with various thrill rides, it also had some educational displays, as well as theatrical productions—mostly of a moralistic nature! The attractions included a small scenic railroad that ran through various landscapes to amuse and entertain the passengers.

Right Luna Park was a colorful attraction that really became magical at night. Even well-dressed ladies enjoyed the slightly risqué fun of "Drop the Dip."

1907: "Drop the Dip," Coney Island, NY

When "Drop the Dip" opened in 1907 it was considered sensational, and to many represents the first true roller coaster, where high speed thrills were the primary aim of the ride.

It was operated at many different locations around the Brooklyn, New York area, but the first variant was destroyed by fire just over a month after it opened. The designer and constructor, Christopher Feucht, rebuilt it, and while he was doing so he made many minor improvements, something that he continued to do for many years. The ride was moved several times, and when it was installed at Luna Park in 1924, its name was changed to "Trip to the Moon." Among other innovative features, it was also notable for the first use of a lapbar.

Status	Removed
Opening date	June 6, 1907
Closing date	1930s
Type	Wooden sitdown
Manufacturer	Arthur Jarvis
Designer	Christopher Feucht, Welcome Mosley
Height	60 ft (18 m)
Duration	1 min 30 sec

1910: "Racer," Sandusky, OH

The roller coaster called "Racer" was an early wooden sit-down racing ride that first opened in 1910. It was designed and built by Fred Ingersoll of Pittsburgh, whose company built near 300 roller coasters in his 25-year long career. He used two sets of wooden rails on top of a trestle frame that sequentially rose and fell as it progressed along an out and back layout. Even though tickets were cheap, however, it was removed from service in 1928 due to a lack of riders, mostly caused by the economic depression.

Status	Removed
Opening date	1910
Closing date	1928
Type	Wooden racing
Manufacturer	McKay Construction
Designer	Fred Ingersoll
Height	46 feet (14 m)

Eleven trains of one car: four riders per train

Opened in 1870 as a beer garden, Cedar Point is the second-oldest amusement park in the United States after Lake Compounce. This is "Racer," an out and back design.

1912: "Scenic Railway," Melbourne, Australia

Status	Operational
Opening date	December 13, 1912
Owner	Linfox, Virtual Communities, and Liberty Petrol
Type	Wooden brakeman
Operating season	All year round
Rides	20
Roller coasters	Two

The "Scenic Railway" opened at Australia's Luna Park in Melbourne, Victoria, Australia in December 1912, which as it is still operating, makes it the oldest continually operating roller coaster in the world. The site where it is located—Luna Park, is an amusement ground on the coast of Port Phillip Bay in St. Kilda.

When the ride was first constructed, the track which is 3,172 feet (967 m) long, used a vast amount of Oregon pine which had to be shipped all the way from Canada. It needed 215,465 feet (65,674 m) in total. Each of the trains weighs nearly two tonnes and they achieve top speeds of about 37 mph (60 km/h).

Right The striking entrance to Luna Park, Melbourne gets the mood exactly right for retro excitement.

1913: "Derby Racer," Cleveland, OH

The "Derby Racer" at Euclid Beach Park was designed by John A. Miller and opened for business in 1913. Cleverly designed, it was state-of-the-art at the time, and ran under this name until 1921 when it was retitled "Racing Coaster" to avoid confusion with another similarly named amusement ride—the park had seven different roller coasters during its lifetime, the first dating from 1896. The "Racing Coaster" continued in use until the park closed in 1969.

Euclid Beach Park—located on the shores of Lake Erie—was inaugurated in 1894, and from 1901 was run by a Cleveland businessman named Dudley S. Humphrey II and his family. They imposed a series of strict dress codes and other regulations to give the establishment a respectable, clean family atmosphere.

Below The layout of "Derby Racer" appeared at first glance to be composed of two parallel tracks, however, there was actually only one; it gave this impression because it was laid out in the form of a Moebius loop.

Below Left The old entrance survived the closure of the park and was designated a historic landmark in 1973.

1914: "Jack Rabbit Derby Racer," East Grand Rapids, MI

The "Jack Rabbit Derby Racer" was a double wooden-track roller coaster (one of only two in the entire United States) with an 80 percent drop. It was owned and built in 1914 by brothers John J. and James McElwee.

It was sited at Ramona Park, an amusement park that first opened in 1897 and operated until 1995. It was a "trolley park," operated by by the Grand Rapids Street Railway Company.

Trolley parks were so called as they were placed at the terminus of a trolley line to stimulate traffic. Romona Park had a theater, the Ramona Gardens Pavilion (which also served as a roller-skating rink), concession stands, and a number of rides—a Ferris wheel, bumper cars, aeroswings, a merry-go-round, and mystic chutes.

The "Jack Rabbit Derby Racer" was initially known as "Ingersoll's Derby Racer," but was renamed shortly after construction. It featured a large drop that was configured at about 80 degrees, making it quite an exceptional experience for the age—this added considerably to its popularity. The coaster was withdrawn from use after forty seasons when the park closed in 1955 to be turned into housing and a shopping center.

Status	Removed
Opening date	1914
Closing date	1955
Type	Double wooden-track
Manufacturer	John J. & James McElwee

Right "Jack Rabbit Derby Racer" was constructed from long-leaf yellow pine, (chosen for durability) and fastened together by nuts and bolts. Most of the construction crews were employees of the trolley company, which owned the park. The track was checked daily with crew members tightening bolts and replacing damaged wood when required. It was easily the most popular ride at the park.

206. DERBY RACER, RAMONA PARK, GRAND RAPIDS, MICH.

1920–1929: THE GOLDEN AGE

The "Twenties" were a golden age for theme parks—by the end of the decade, there were about 2,000 rides underway in the USA alone. This was for a number of reasons, including a general desire to throw off the bad memories of both the First World War and the crippling influenza pandemic that followed. Between the two tragedies, millions of lives had been lost.

People were also getting more leisure time as well as earning a bit more, and amusement parks were a fashionable way of getting out and about with family and friends. Safety had come on by leaps and bounds, with such things as wheels that locked to the tracks, while anti-runaway emergency brakes had become a commonplace feature.

Below Left Even though the "Scenic Railway" at Cedar Point had been around for a long time, it had been rebuilt in 1918 and remained a popular ride. This image was taken in about 1920.

Below "Razzle Dazzle" was one of the earliest attractions at Coney Island. This photograph dates from around the turn of the 20th century.

SCENIC RAILWAY
ABOUT 1920

RAZZLE DAZZLE

1922: "Big Dipper," San Francisco, CA

Status	Removed
Opening date	1922
Closing date	1955
Type	Wood
Manufacturer	Arthur Looff
Designer	Prior & Church

The "Big Dipper" was a legendary roller coaster at what was then called Chutes at the Beach, an amusement park located next to Ocean Beach, on the western edge of San Francisco. In 1929 it was renamed Playland at the Beach after it was taken over by George and Leo Whitney. It was conveniently situated to draw large crowds from the city.

The "Big Dipper" was constructed over a period of two months as a replacement for an old figure of eight ride which was demolished to make room. Opening in 1922, it quickly became the park's main attraction, although there were many accidents, including one in 1945 when a passenger was killed when he stood up at speed and hit his head on one of the support beams.

Left "Big Dipper" was in constant use until 1955 when a mix of new regulations and declining passenger numbers made it uneconomic to continue operating.

1924: "Thunderbolt," West Mifflin, PA

Status	Operating
Opening date	1924 (as "Pippin")
	1968 (as "Thunderbolt")
Type	Wood
Designer	Andy Vettel & John A. Miller
Track layout	Terrain
Height	70 ft (21 m)
Drop	95 ft (29 m)
Length	2,887 ft (880 m)
Speed	55 mph (89 km/h)
Duration	1 min 41sec

Three trains of four cars. Riders two x three rows: 24 riders a train

Right "Thunderbolt" was rated by the *New York Times* in 1974 as the number one roller coaster in the whole United States.

"Thunderbolt," which is a wooden roller coaster that was built in 1924 by John A. Miller, was originally called "Pippin." Its name was changed to its current moniker at the beginning of the 1968 season because the ride had been updated and extended to become more thrilling—thanks to the work of a team led by designer Andy Vettel. It is sited at Kennywood Park in West Mifflin, near Pittsburgh, one of six roller coasters at the site.

The "King of Coasters" layout is of the terrain type, taking advantage of natural features such as ravines to make the ride experience more exciting—with drops at the beginning and end of the ride.

1925: "Cyclone," Revere, MA

The "Cyclone" was a popular wooden roller coaster that first opened in 1925 at Revere Beach—the first public beach in the United States, developed at the end of the Boston, Revere Beach & Lynn Railroad.

The "Cyclone" was designed by Frederick Church and built by Harry Traver of Traver Engineering, and went on to have a long and illustrious career, including setting many records as well as being damaged by floods, storms, and blizzards. Despite surviving all these extreme weather events, it was eventually destroyed by another cataclysm—fire—in March 1974 and then finally demolished the following month. For nearly forty years it was rated as the tallest coaster in the world, being the first to surpass 100 feet (30 m) in height—this reign ended in 1964 when a taller structure was in Mexico. It may well have also been the fastest coaster in the world for some time.

Status	Removed
Opening date	1925
Closing date	1969 (fire)
Demolished	April 1974
Type	Wood
Cost	$125,000
Manufacturer	Traver Engineering
Designer	Frederick Church
Height	100 ft (30 m)
Length	3,600 ft (1,100 m)
Speed	45 mph (72 km/h)
Capacity	1,400 riders per hour

Left "Cyclone" quickly earned a reputation as a dangerous ride: on only the second day of operation, a woman fell from her seat and died. In those less sensitive times, the ride reopened 20 minutes after her body was recovered.

1925: "Giant Dipper," San Diego, CA

Status	Operating
Opening date	July 4, 1925
Type	Wooden twister
Manufacturer & Designer	Frank Prior, Fredrick Church
Lift/launch system	Chain lift hill
Height	73 ft (22 m)
Drop	60 ft (18 m)
Length	2,600 ft (790 m)
Speed	55 mph (89 km/h)
Duration	1 min 45 sec

Trains of six cars. Riders two x two rows: twenty-four riders a train

Left "Giant Dipper" has had various name changes over the years—it began life as "Earthquake," then became simply "Roller Coaster," before finally becoming "Giant Dipper."

The "Giant Dipper" is a wooden roller coaster that is sometimes also referred to as the "Mission Beach Roller Coaster." It is located on a small amusement site at Belmont Park, in Mission Beach, San Diego, California.

Built in 1925 it is one of only two surviving rides by renowned designers Frank Prior and Frederick Church. The other—also named "Giant Dipper"—is at the Santa Cruz Beach Boardwalk. Although the San Diego ride came close to being demolished in 1978, it was given legal protection as the result of being placed on the National Register of Historic Places. In 1986 it was also made a National Historic Landmark.

1926: "Crystal Beach Cyclone," Fort Erie, Canada

Status	Demolished
Opening date	1927
Closing date	1946
Type	Wooden twister
Cost	$176,000
Manufacturer	Traver Engineering
Designer	Harry G. Traver
Lift/launch system	Chain-lift hill
Height	96 ft (29 m)
Drop	90 ft (27 m)
Length	2,953 ft (900 m)
Speed	60 mph (97 km/h)
Duration	40 sec
G-force	4 Gs

One/two trains of three cars depending on demand. Riders x four: twelve riders per train

Right A nurse was kept on permanent duty to attend to victims of dizziness and fainting after experiencing the notorious "Crystal Beach Cyclone" thrill ride.

The "Crystal Beach Cyclone" which opened in 1927 was one of three notoriously extreme roller coasters designed and built by Harry G. Traver in the late 1920s. It featured a twisted layout with lots of banked turns and sudden drops as well as figure of eight sections—and almost no straight lengths of track. The ride was sited in the Crystal Beach Amusement Park which survived for a century: 1888 to 1989.

Although the "Crystal Beach Cyclone" had been a very popular attraction in its time, it fell victim to the wartime gloom of the early 1940s when amusement parks became unfashionable and people largely stopped going. As a result, the Cyclone proved uneconomic to maintain and it was withdrawn from service in 1946 and then later dismantled.

1927: "Cyclone," Coney Island, NY

Status	Operating
Opening date	June 26, 1927
Type	Wooden twister
Cost	$175,000
Designer	Vernon Keenan
Lift/launch system	Chain-lift
Height	85 ft (26 m)
Length	2,850 ft (869 m)
Speed	60 mph (97 km/h)
Duration	2 min 30 sec
G-force	3.75 Gs

Three trains of three cars. Riders two x four rows: twenty-four riders a train

The "Cyclone"—also known as the "Coney Island Cyclone" to distinguish it from other rides—was opened to the public on June 26, 1927. It is a wooden coaster that has managed to survive despite plans by the civic authorities to scrap it in the 1970s. Fortunately, instead of being torn down, it was refurbished and put back into operation on July 3, 1975. On its sixty-fourth birthday (June 26,1991) it was named a National Historic Landmark. Since 2012, 2,400 of its 2,800 feet of track have been replaced to ensure safety.

Left "Cyclone" is one of the most famous thrill rides in the world, because it has featured in many movies and TV shows.

1930–1939: THE DEPRESSION

The 1930s were a desperate time for many people, but the situation was particularly bad in the USA where the Great Depression was biting hard.

The number of roller coasters being operated acted as a good barometer of the times—in 1930, for instance, there were somewhere approaching 2,000, but by 1935, this had crashed to slightly over 300, and by 1939 it had plummeted even further, to just under 250. By then only two manufacturing companies—the Philadelphia Toboggan Company and National Amusement Devices still made them.

Above Long Beach, California, amusement park and pier as it was in the 1930s.

1934: "Blue Flyer," Blackpool, UK

Status	Operating
Opening date	1934 as "Zipper Dipper"
	2011 as "Blue Flyer"
Type	Wood
Designer	Charlie Paige
Height	25 ft (7.6 m)
Length	2,293 ft. (699 m)
Speed	25 mph (40 km/h)
Duration	1 min

Ten car trains: riders x two across: twenty riders a train

"Blue Flyer" is a wooden family roller coaster that was formerly known as both "Zipper Dipper" and "Warburtons Milk Roll-A-Coaster." The latest name was applied after the ride was rethemed to coincide with the opening of Nickelodeon Land on May 4, 2011.

Historic England gives it a Grade II listing as one of only six pre-WWII roller coasters in the UK and the second-oldest children's coaster in the world. (The oldest is the 1927 Kiddie Coaster at Playland Park, NY.) It was originally constructed in 1934, by the Dayton Fun House, overseen by Charlie Paige. The train, which was built by Philadelphia Toboggan Coasters, has five cars with four seats in each, meaning it can carry a total of 20 passengers.

1938: "Rollo Coaster," Ligonier, PA

Status	Operating
Opening date	1938
Type	Wooden out and back
Manufacturer	Philadelphia Toboggan Coasters
Designer	Herbert Paul Schmeck
Lift/launch system	Chain lift
Height	27 ft (8.2 m)
Drop	25 ft (7.6 m)
Length	900 ft (270 m)
Speed	25 mph (40 km/h)
Duration	1 min 15 sec

Originally two trains of three cars holding 12; since refurbishment reduced to 10

"Rollo Coaster" is an out and back wooden roller coaster that was built in 1938 by Philadelphia Toboggan Coasters and located at Idlewild and Soak Zone near Ligonier. It has recently reopened after two years refurbishment following an accident. Philadelphia Toboggan Coasters—still going strong!—manufactured a new train with more safety features.

Left Designed to exploit the naturally steep terrain, "Rollo Coaster" follows hills and gullies to maximum effect, giving the passengers a feeling of real speed.

1940–1949: THE DECLINE

Although the long years of the Great Depression had already obliterated much of the amusement industry, the outbreak of World War II brought on a period of austerity during the 1940s that made things considerably worse.

A lot of the parks that had managed to survive through the Depression either closed down later, or came close to it. One of the few exceptions was Dodge Park Playland at Council Bluffs, Iowa, which opened up in 1948.

1940: Centennial Exhibition,
Wellington, New Zealand

The Centennial Exhibition was staged in Rongotai, Wellington in 1940, and its popularity is little short of amazing—in a country that only had a population of 1.6 million people, over 2.6 million actually visited.

Although the main purpose of the event was to showcase the country's strengths and exhibit displays of science, culture, and industry, the area called Playland attracted vast numbers of attendees. This was where the amusements were located, including a Crazy House and a roller coaster. After the exhibition closed the site was used to house Air Force personnel and then for storage, before burning down in 1946.

Opposite This postcard dates from about 1949, and shows the front entrance of Playland with its roller coaster looming enticingly behind. The styling clearly proclaims its Art Deco modernity and all the exciting glamor of the age.

Far Left The roller coaster at the New Zealand Centennial Exhibition. Photo by Eric Lee-Johnson.

Left The New Zealand Centennial Exhibition was held between November 1939 and May 4, 1940, just after the Second World War started, but it was still a big success.

Chapter Four: The Future Starts

Two women having a great time on the roller coaster ride at the State Fair of Dallas, Texas, in September 1954.

1950–1959: A NEW BEGINNING

Amusement parks continued to do badly through the first half of the 1950s, but this decline was reversed when Walt Disney opened Disneyland in Anaheim in July 1955. Other businesses soon followed his lead.

Left Postcard of the "Giant Roller Coaster" at Lagoon, Fun Spot of Utah.

Below Young boy and girl waiting for the train to load in Toronto, c. 1950. Note the complete lack of safety features!

1950: "Little Dipper," Melrose Park, IL

Status	Closed
Opening date	1950
Closed	September 27, 2009
Relocated	Six Flags Great America in 2010
Type	Wooden junior
Manufacturer	Philadelphia Toboggan Coasters
Designer	Herbert Schmeck
Lift/launch system	Chain lift hill
Height	28 ft (8.5 m)
Drop	24 ft (7.3 m)
Length	700 ft (210 m)
Speed	25 mph (40 km/h)
Duration	50 sec

One train of four cars. Riders two x two rows: sixteen riders a train

Left Bought at auction by Six Flags Great America, "Little Dipper" was relocated to their site in Gurnee, Illinois where it reopened on May 27, 2010—and continues to excite its passengers.

"Little Dipper" is a wooden roller coaster that originally operated at Kiddieland Amusement Park. Kiddieland was opened by Arthur E. Fritz in 1929. It was a gentle amusement site with a number of rides including a Ferris wheel, miniature steam locos, a carousel, and, from 1950, "Little Dipper." It was manufactured by Philadelphia Toboggan Coasters and ran successfully until 2009 when the park was closed after the landowners refused to extend the lease. The much-loved figure-eight track was purchased for $33,000 by Six Flags Great America and now can be found north of Chicago.

1951: "Vuoristorata," Helsinki, Finland

Originally built as a temporary structure to attract crowds to the 1952 Summer Olympics in Helsinki, "Vuoristorata" proved popular enough to keep running after it finished. Due to a combination of the harsh environment it is located in, and a careful maintenance routine, every piece of wood on the entire coaster has been replaced at least five times over the duration of its lifetime.

The ride was designed by Valdemar Lebeck and opened in 1951, but was actually a close copy of another one he'd created in 1932 in Denmark, called "Rutschebanen." For many years they were the highest roller coasters in Europe. These days "Vuoristorata" is considered to be a permanent feature of the park and its future is secure. The capacity of the ride is touted as 1,320 people an hour.

Status	Operating
Opening date	July 13, 1951
Type	Wooden side-friction
Cost	48,000,000 FIM
Manufacturer	Svend Jarlström
Designer	Valdemar Lebech
Lift/launch system	Cable lift hill
Height	75.2 ft (22.9 m)
Drop	75 ft (23 m)
Length	3,149.6 ft (960 m)
Speed	37.3 mph (60 km/h)
Duration	2 min 10 sec

Four trains of four cars. Riders two x three rows: twenty-four riders a train

Left "Vuoristorata" ("roller coaster" in Finnish) is a wooden side-friction coaster located in Linnanmäki amusement park. Linnanmäki translates from Finnish into English as "Mountain range track."

1951: "Comet," Erie, PA

Status	Operating
Opening date	1951
Type	Wooden junior
Manufacturer	Philadelphia Toboggan Coasters
Designer	Herbert Paul Schmeck
Lift/launch system	Chain
Height	37 ft (11 m)
Drop	25 ft (7.6 m)
Length	1,300 ft (400 m)
Speed	25 mph (40 km/h)
Duration	1 min 24 sec

One train of four cars. Riders two x two rows: Sixteen riders a train

Right "Comet" gives almost exactly the same gently thrilling ride today as it did on the day it opened in 1951.

Waldameer Park was a trolley park, developed at the terminus of the Erie Electric Motor Company from 1896. Today it is one of the few still running, extended in 1986 to include Waterworld. It has seen considerable expansion and has over 30 rides.

"Comet" is a wooden junior roller coaster that was built in 1951 and is still in operation, was designed by Herbert Schmeck and manufactured by the Philadelphia Toboggan Company and laid out in a multilevel figure of eight configuration, but with more elevated tracks than previous similar models. It reaches a maximum height of 37 feet (11 m), and features a drop of 25 feet (7.6 m), as well as several bunny hops over the course of more than 1,300 feet (400 m) of track.

1956: "Sea Dragon," Powell, OH

Opened	1956
Closed	2006
Type	Wooden junior figure of eight
Manufacturer	Philadelphia Toboggan Coasters
Designer	John C. Allen
Lift/launch system	Chain lift hill
Height	35 ft (10.6 m)
Length	1,320 ft (400 m)
Speed	25 mph (40 km/h)
Duration	1 min 30 sec
Max vertical angle	45 degrees

Two trains of four cars. Riders two x two rows: sixteen riders a train

"Sea Dragon" is the oldest operating junior wooden roller coaster in Ohio. Originally called "Jet Flyer," it was opened in 1956 in the Wyandot Lake Amusement Park. The park was acquired by the Colombus Zoo and Aquarium in 2006. "Sea Dragon"is still running along a figure-eight, double out and back track that starts at the tall lift hill. The brakes in the curved station are applied manually with hand-controlled levers.

Left In 2006 the park split into two: the dry ride area became Jungle Jack's Landing while the water park became known as Zoombezi Bay.

1958: "Wooden Roller Coaster," Vancouver, Canada

Status	Operating
Opened	1958
Type	Wood
Cost	$200,000
Designer	Carl Phare, Walker LeRoy
Lift/launch system	Chain lift hill
Height	68 ft (21 m)
Length	2,840 ft (870 m)
Speed	45 mph (72 km/h)

Three trains of eight cars. Riders two x four rows: 16 riders per train

The oldest thrill ride in Canada and one of the top wooden roller coasters in the world, Wooden Roller Coaster, is located at Playland, British Columbia. It was built board-by-board, and opened in 1958 at which time it was the largest roller coaster in the country. At this time it cost riders 40 cents a go. The ride boasts a 75 foot (23 m) first drop, then numerous twists and turns, air-time hills, and camel hops, plus a classic fan curve. The ride is constantly inspected and every effort is made to retain the original wood wherever possible. When it rains in winter, the wood swells and the ride is a little slower, but in summer when the sun shrinks the timbers the ride speeds up. Each of its three trains use eight open-front, single bench, flange-wheeled cars.

1960–1969: AMUSEMENT PARKS

While Walt Disney's revival of the amusement industry in the 1950s had the effect of enthusing other businessmen to invest in new parks, a lot of the others did little to update their facilities. As a result the outdated sites stagnated during the 1960s, causing many of them to shut down. This included such places as Riverview Park in Chicago, Illinois, which closed its doors for the last time in 1967.

At the other end of the spectrum were institutions like the Busch Gardens Tampa and the first of the Six Flags chain which started in 1960. This period also saw the introduction of many new thrill rides, including the first log flumes, as well as runaway mine trains.

As a case study, Pacific Park on Santa Monica Pier, opened in 1909—initially as just a municipal facility with no amusements. Over the years it was amalgamated with an adjacent structure called the Pleasure Pier, and became the site of many family attractions. It felt the grip of financial pressures in the 1960s—but somehow managed to survive, despite the threat to demolish the pier on which it is housed.

Left Riders enjoying the roller coaster at Riverview Amusement Park in July 1950.

Right Santa Monica Pier is home to 12 rides, including the only solarpowered Ferris wheel (called "Pacific Wheel"), and an extensive steel roller coaster that runs around the perimeter of the pier.

1964: "Blue Streak," Sandusky, Ohio

Status	Operating
Opened	May 23, 1964
Type	Wooden out and back
Cost	$200,000
Manufacturer	Philadelphia Toboggan Coasters
Designer	Frank F. Hoover & John C. Allen
Lift/launch system	Chain lift hill
Height	78 ft (24 m)
Drop	72 ft (22 m)
Length	2,558 ft (780 m)
Speed	40 mph (64 km/h)
Duration	1 min 45 sec

Two trains of four cars. Riders two x three rows: 24 riders a train

Right "Blue Streak" opened for business in 1964 and is the oldest roller coaster in the park.

"Blue Streak" is a popular wooden roller coaster that has been consistently highly rated by worldwide enthusiasts since it opened—helping make Cedar Point the most visited seasonal park in the United States (of course the park's great views of Lake Erie also help). "Blue Streak" isn't the longest ride in the park—four of the rides break 2 min 30 sec—but for an old ride it's certainly worth standing in line.

1967: "Cannon Ball," Georgia, TN

Status	Operating
Opening date	1967
Type	Wooden out and back
Manufacturer	Philadelphia Toboggan Coasters
Designer	John C. Allen
Lift/launch system	Chain lift hill
Height	70 ft (21 m)
Drop	70 ft (21 m)
Length	2,272 ft (693 m)
Speed	50 mph (80 km/h)
Duration	1 min 32 sec

Two trains of three cars. Riders two x three rows: eighteen riders a train

"Cannon Ball" is a wooden roller coaster at Lake Winnepesaukah amusement park in Rossville. Lake Winnie opened on June 1, 1925, and today boasts two more roller coasters, four water rides, the unique "Fly-O-Plane," the 140 ft "Oh-Zone" drop tower, and the more recent "Twister," as well as a 1916 carousel.

Although "Cannon Ball" doesn't break any records for height—rising only 70 feet (21 m)—it is a classic roller coaster and provides a great ride, making it one of the main attractions at the site.

Below "Cannon Ball" may be old but it's a great family ride with plenty of airtime.

1969: "Cedar Creek Mine Ride," Sandusky, OH

Status	Operating
Opening date	May 24, 1969
Type	Steel mine train
Manufacturer	Arrow Dynamics
Designer	Ron Toomer
Lift/launch system	Two chain lift hills
Height	48 ft (15 m)
Length	2,540 ft (770 m)
Speed	42 mph (68 km/h)
Duration	2 min 42 sec

Four trains of five cars. Riders two x three rows: 30 riders a train

"Cedar Creek Mine Ride" is a multilift hill mine train roller coaster manufactured for Cedar Point amusement park, where it opened in 1969. Since that time it has excited tens of millions of riders who travel in trains which can carry up to thirty passengers at a time.

It is a steel coaster on wooden supports, themed to the Gold Rush era, giving Wild West excitement as a runaway mine train rushing up and down hills, over water, and through a tunnel before coming to a helix finish.

Right "Cedar Creek Mine Ride" is mostly wooden but has a steel track which runs along a series of small bumps leading up to a helix ending.

1970–1979: FALL & RISE

In the early 1970s, the collapse of several older style amusement parks continued as newer ones proved more attractive to the paying public. Palisades Amusement Park, for instance, had not moved with the times, and even though it was located in New Jersey, just across the Hudson River from New York City, it could not compete with more exciting alternatives, and closed down in 1971.

What thrill-seekers wanted were good quality rides, and their wishes were certainly met as more roller coasters were built between 1974 and 1980 than had been created since the Golden Years of the 1920s. The famous designer Ron Toomer typified the new way of doing things, and among his innumerable successes was the "Corkscrew" ride at Knott's Berry Farm at Buena Park, California, which opened on May 21, 1975. This was the first steel inverting roller coaster of the modern era, and was the first of ten exact replicas, all of which were very highly rated by their excited and thrilled passengers.

Right The roller coaster "Revolution," at Six Flags Magic Mountain, opened on May 8, 1976 and boasted the first successful vertical loop.

1970: "Jet Star," Seaside Heights, NJ

Status	Removed
Opening date	1970
Closing date	2000
Type	Steel
Manufacturer	Anton Schwarzkopf
Height	44.3 ft (13.5 m)
Length	1,765.1 ft (538 m)
Speed	31.1 mph (50 km/h)

Four cars. Riders 2 x 2 rows.

"Jet Star" was a steel roller coaster that came with a wild reputation. Thrill-seekers found it at Casino Pier in Seaside Heights. It operated from 1970 to 2000 and was then replaced by "Star Jet." The latter was later destroyed by Hurricane Sandy in October 2012 when the boardwalk was partially destroyed and the coaster ignominiously dumped into the Atlantic waves—where it stayed for seven months until it was disposed of in May 2013.

Left Although "Jet Star" wasn't particularly high—only 44 feet—it was considered to be an extreme ride due to the viciousness of the drops and the G-forces imposed by high-speed cornering. When the pier and boardwalk were refurbished and extended, the ride was replaced with "Hydrus."

1972: "The Racer," Mason, OH

Status	Operating
Opening date	April 29, 1972
Cost	$1.2 million
Type	Wooden racing out and back
Manufacturer	Philadelphia Toboggan Coasters
Designer	John C. Allen
Lift/launch system	Chain
Height	88 ft (26.8 m)
Drop	82.17 ft (25 m)
Length	3,415 ft (1,041 m)
Speed	53 mph (85.3 km/h)
Duration	2 min

Four trains of five cars. Riders two x three rows: 30 riders per train

Left "The Racer" claimed to be the fastest roller coaster in the world when it opened.

When it was built in 1972, "The Racer" was unlike any other out and back wooden racing coaster in existence and is credited with starting off the second great age of thrill rides. Unlike conventional types, Allen laid it out so that the tracks—which started out parallel—then separated onto different structures before rejoining again just before the finish. This novel aspect was so popular that it soon appeared at other amusement parks on other coasters.

1973: "Great American Scream Machine," Atlanta, GA

Status	Operating
Opening date	March 31, 1973
Type	Wooden out and back
Manufacturer	Philadelphia Toboggan Coasters
Designer	Don Rosser, John C. Allen, William Cobb
Lift/launch system	Chain lift hill
Height	105 ft (32 m)
Drop	89 ft (27 m)
Length	3,800 ft (1,200 m)
Speed	57 mph (92 km/h)
Duration	2 min
G-force	3.7 Gs

Two trains of four cars. Riders two x three rows: 24 riders a train

There were two "Great American Scream Machines"—this one, which is still operating, located at Six Flags Over Georgia and constructed of wood, and another at Six Flags Great Adventure in Jackson, New Jersey, made of steel.

The New Jersey ride—a bumpy one—lasted from 1989 till 2010 when it was removed and replaced by "Green Lantern." The Atlanta version opened in 1973 when it was the tallest, fastest, and longest roller coaster of its time. It featured eleven drops and when it was first built the trains were controlled manually. These days "Great American Scream Machines" has been completely computerized and is painted in patriotic red, white, and blue.

Right For a limited period of the 2018 season the "Great American Scream Machine" ran backwards over the track: this had happened before in the early 1990s. Six Flags Over Georgia is nearly 300-acres in size with over forty rides and celebrated its fiftieth birthday on June 16, 2017.

1975: "Canobie Corkscrew," Salem, NH

The "Canobie Corkscrew," which is a steel sit-down roller coaster, has had two previous incarnations. When it first opened in 1975, it was called "Chicago Loop" and was sited at an indoor amusement park at Old Chicago in Bolingbrook, Illinois. When the park closed in 1980, it was relocated to Alabama State Fairgrounds where it ran as "Corkscrew." After that, it was bought by Canobie Lake Park in Salem, New Hampshire, in 1986, where it is still operating. The ride features a single drop that flows into a 180-degree banked turn which then feeds into a double corkscrew.

Status	Operating
Opening date	1975 (Chicago Loop)
	1982 (Corkscrew)
	1987 (Canobie Lake Corkscrew)
Type	Steel corkscrew
Manufacturer	Arrow Development
Lift/launch system	Chain lift hill
Height	73 ft (22 m)
Speed	45 mph (72 km/h)
Inversions	Two
Duration	1 min 30 sec

Trains of six cars. Riders two x two rows: twenty-four riders a train

Left The "Canobie Corkscrew" is an ideal introduction to thrill rides. It is a steel roller coaster that features one large drop and two fairly gentle corkscrew loops. There are ten thrill rides at Canobie Lake Park, from the traditional wooden "Yankee Cannonball" to the "Extreme Frisbee."

1976: "Corkscrew," Sandusky, OH

Status	Operating
Opening date	May 15, 1976
Type	Steel custom looping out and back
Manufacturer	Arrow
Designer	Ron Toomer
Height	85 ft (26 m)
Drop	65 ft (20 m)
Length	2,050 ft (620 m)
Speed	48 mph (77 km/h)
Inversions	Three
Duration	2 min

Three trains of six cars. Riders two x two rows; twenty-four riders a train

"Corkscrew" is a steel roller coaster that opened in 1976 at Cedar Point—the self-proclaimed Roller Coaster Capital of the World. It was the first coaster in existence to include three inversions, and was also constructed with the first vertical loop that Arrow had ever manufactured—but was beaten to the record books by "Revolution" at Magic Mountain. The ride spreads over five acres and, inspired by the US Bicentennial—the same year as it was constructed—as can be seen in the photo at left, the track is blue, the supports white—but what can't be seen here is that the cars are red.

1978: "Loch Ness Monster," Williamsburg, PA

The "Loch Ness Monster" is a steel roller coaster that is named after the legendary Scottish beast that is said to inhabit the waters of the infamous loch. It is appropriately located in Busch Gardens' Scottish-themed area called Heatherdown. It was designed by Ron Toomer and its 55-degree drop was the steepest in the world when it opened.

Status	Operating
Opening date	June 6, 1978
Type	Steel custom looping terrain
Manufacturer	Arrow Development
Designer	Ron Toomer
Lift/launch system	Two chain lift hills
Height	130 ft (40 m)
Drop	114 ft (35 m)
Length	3,240 ft (990 m)
Speed	60 mph (97 km/h)
Inversions	Two
Duration	2 min 10 sec
G-force	3.5 Gs

Trains of seven cars. Riders two x two rows: twenty-eight riders a train

Left The "Loch Ness Monster" opened to the public in 1978 when it was considered to be both the world's tallest and fastest roller coaster. It is one of only two complete-circuit roller coasters with two interlocking loops—and as "Orient Express" at Worlds of Fun in Kansas, Missouri is now closed, it is the only surviving coaster like this. Its fortieth birthday in 2018 saw its fifty-eighth million passenger.

1979: "The Beast," Cincinnati, OH

Status	Operating
Opening date	April 14, 1979
Type	Wooden terrain
Cost	$4 million
Manufacturer	Kings Island
Designers	Al Collins, Jeff Gramke, and John C. Allen
Lift/launch system	Two chain lift hills
Height	110 ft (34 m)
Drop	141 ft (43 m)
Length	7,359 ft (2,243 m)
Speed	64.78 mph (104 km/h)
Duration	4 min 10 sec
G-force	3.6 Gs

Three trains of six cars. Riders two x three rows: thirty-six riders a train

"The Beast" is a notorious wooden roller coaster that broke all manner of records when it opened in 1979—at the time it was the fastest, tallest, and longest wooden roller coaster in the world—and still holds the latter record. It is arranged over 35 acres (14 hectares), exploiting the up and down nature of the surrounding topography to enhance the ride experience.

After two years of intensive research and design, "The Beast" was built in-house over the period of a year in the mid 1970s. The bare statistics of the construction are awesome—650,000 feet of southern pine wood, 37,500 lbs of nails, 82,480 bolts and washers, and 2,432 square yards of concrete—all to build 1.4 miles of track that feature stomach-churning 45-degree vertical dives of 135 feet, plus another of 18 degrees and 141 feet, then a 125-foot tunnel, eight banked turns of up to 45 degrees, and then a 540-degree helix tunnel near the finish.

Left It is estimated that each of the three trains of "The Beast" of Cincinnati has traveled over 898,000 miles—the equivalent of 35 times around the world! This also equates to over 52 million rides, making Kings Island the third most visited park ever. "The Beast" is many thrill ride connoisseurs most favorite ride ever—anywhere.

1980–1989: REINCARNATION

The 1980s saw a boom in the number of visitors to amusement parks—this was primarily because people knew that the rides they could go on were worth traveling distance for.

Although wooden coaster design had more or less reached its peak, this was not the case with steel models which continued to push the boundaries of physics and engineering throughout the decade. This included everything from banked tracks and multiple inversions, to suspended and inverted coasters, stand-up trains, and the first of the Vekoma Boomerangs. New records were being set all the time, as typified by Ron Toomer's "Magnum XL-200," which, located at Cedar Point in Ohio, was the first coaster to pass the 200 feet (60 m) high mark.

Left Expo '86 ran from May to October 1986 in Vancouver, British Columbia, Canada and was the showcase for the latest technological advances, particularly for the transport world. One of the highlights was "Scream Machine," a steel custom made, double corkscrew ride. The original manufacturer was Arrow Dynamics but the company fell into bankruptcy and the contract was taken up by Vekoma. After the show closed the ride was relocated to Six Flags St Louis as "Ninja."

1980: "Carolina Cyclone," Charlotte, NC

The "Carolina Cyclone" is a steel roller coaster built by Arrow Dynamics that opened in March, 1980. At the time it cost two million dollars to construct—this was mostly because of the complex structure, it being the first ever ride to feature four inversions, two loops, and two corkscrews. It is located at Carowinds in Charlotte, North Carolina, and is still operating, although in 2010 it had a thorough makeover in the form of a differently colored paint scheme—something that has been done numerous times before.

Status	Operating
Opening date	March 1980
Type	Steel
Cost	$2 million
Manufacturer	Arrow Dynamics
Designer	Ron Toomer
Lift/launch system	Chain lift hill
Height	95 ft (29 m)
Drop	65 ft (20 m)
Length	2,100 ft (640 m)
Speed	41 mph (66 km/h)
Inversions	Four
Duration	1 min 30 sec
G-force	3.5 Gs

Two trains of seven cars. Riders two x two rows; twenty-eight riders a train

Left The "Carolina Cyclone" lives up to its name with speeds of 41 mph and roars its riders through two 360 degree vertical loops barrel rolls, then two 360 degree barrel-rolls, then and a 450 degree uphill helix over the midway.

"The Mindbender," Edmonton, Canada

Status	Operating
Opening date	1985
Type	Steel twister
Manufacturer	Anton Schwarzkopf
Designer	Werner Stengel
Track layout	Indoor Twister
Lift/launch system	Chain lift hill
Height	145 ft (44 m)
Drop	127 ft (38.7 m)
Length	4,198 ft (1,279.5 m)
Speed	60 mph (96.5 km/h)
Inversions	Three
Duration	1 min 13 sec
G-force	5.2 Gs

Two trains of three cars. Riders two x two rows: 12 riders a train

"The Mindbender," which was designed by Werner Stengel and built by Anton Schwarzkopf, is the world's largest indoor triple-loop roller coaster. You can find it at Galaxyland Amusement Park, West Edmonton Mall, in Edmonton, Alberta, Canada.

Based on an earlier ride of Stengel's called "Dreier Looping," "The Mindbender" is taller and has more spirals at the finish. The ride suffered a terrible accident in June 1986 when a wheel broke free, and despite having extensive passenger restraints, four people were thrown 25 feet (7.6 m) to the ground: three of them died. "The Mindbender" was shut down for over a year while it was extensively revamped to improve safety, including the addition of seat belts and headrests. As the second loop allows 5.5Gs, headrests sound like a good idea.

Right "The Mindbender" cars have shoulder restraints that curve over the biceps to prevent riders from putting their arms in the air—there are lots and lots of really close support poles.

1988: "Boomerang," Mexico City, Mexico

Status	Operating
Opening date	1988
Type	Steel boomerang
Manufacturer	Vekoma
Designer	Arrow Dynamics
Height	116.5 ft (35.5 m)
Length	935 ft (285 m)
Speed	47 mph (76 km/h)
Inversions	Three
Duration	1 min 48 sec
G-force	5.2 Gs

One train of seven cars. Riders two x two rows: twenty-eight riders a train

Left The "Boomerang" is a popular thrill ride with park operators—it has a relatively cheap price tag and a small footprint—making it perfect for smaller amusement parks. Its name describes the journey: you get thrown out and—like a boomerang—return to where you started. Unlike a boomerang, however, on this ride you return backwards.

"Boomerang," a roller coaster that is currently operating at Six Flags México, was built to a standard Vekoma Boomerang design that is also found at more than fifty different sites around the world—if you include the "Invertigo," "Giant Inverted," and family versions of the ride.

It was the first of its kind to be built, and was opened to the public in 1984 at Puebla in Mexico. It ran there until 1986, when it was dismantled and reassembled at Reino Aventura, reopening in 1988. It was called "Escorpión" for seven years, but when Six Flags bought the park—reopening in 2000—it went back to being called "Boomerang."

1989: "Magnum XL-200," Sandusky, OH

Status	Operating
Opening date	May 6, 1989
Type	Steel hypercoaster out and back
Cost	$8 million
Manufacturer	Arrow Dynamics
Designer	Ron Toomer
Lift/launch system	Chain lift hill
Height	205 ft (62 m)
Drop	194.7 ft (59.3 m)
Length	5,106 ft (1,556 m)
Speed	72 mph (116 km/h)
Duration	2 min

Three trains of six cars. Riders two x three rows: thirty-six riders a train

Right A new name was needed to describe the white-knuckle extreme ride provided by "Magnum XL-200." The answer was hypercoaster—meaning it is over 200 ft high, with lightning fast speeds, and plenty of air time. 1,450, 892 people enjoyed the thrill in 2017.

"Magnum XL-200" is another steel roller coaster that was designed by Ron Toomer and built by Arrow Dynamics for Cedar Point in Sandusky, Ohio, at a cost of $8 million. As is to be expected, the ride the team came up with broke a number of world records —for a start at over 200 feet (61 m) high, it was the first ever hypercoaster; it was also the fastest, and steepest, complete-circuit roller coaster in existence.

Since it first opened on May 6, 1989, it has carried tens of millions of riders, and in that time has been awarded a multitude of industry and enthusiast awards. The views from it of Lake Erie are extraordinary.

Chapter Five:
Bigger, Better, Faster

"Infusion" opened at Blackpool Pleasure Beach, UK, in 2007. Built by Vekoma, it's 2,260 ft long, has five inversions, reaches nearly 50 mph, and its top height is 109 ft 4 in. It's one of ten roller coasters at the venue, the most recent being Mack Rides' Icon: 2 min 41 sec of extreme pleasure, this is Britain's only double-launch roller coaster at time of writing.

1990–1999: RELOCATION, RESTORATION, & PRESERVATION

The 1990s saw two parallel developments in the roller coaster world—the first and most obvious was a continuation in the building of bigger, better, even faster, rides. The other, and more subtle trend, was the renovation of old coasters—relocating and/or restoring them with the benefit of decent budgets and modern safety systems and standards. By the end of the decade, this had become commonplace across the world, much to the delight of many thrill ride fans.

Not only did the public like many of the old attractions, but it also made financial sense since they were relatively cheap to overhaul. In stark contrast was the fact that in order to compete for any of the big records, parks had to spend tens of millions of dollars to just get even noticed.

Above Santa Monica pier opened early in the twentieth century, and although its amusements stagnated for many years, it has now been brought into the modern era, but still manages to retain much of its old world charm.

1991: "Mean Streak," Sandusky, OH

Status	Removed
Opening date	1991
Closed	2016
Type	Wooden twister
Cost	$7.5 million
Manufacturer	Dinn Corporation
Designer	Curtis D. Summers
Lift/launch system	Chain lift
Height	161 ft (49 m)
Drop	155 ft (47 m)
Length	5,427 ft (1,654 m)
Speed	65 mph (104 km/h)
Duration	3 min 13 sec

Three trains of seven cars. Riders two x two rows: twenty-eight riders a train

Right When "Mean Streak" was closed at the end of the 2016 season, its future was in doubt. Over the next year hints were dropped about its reappearance—finally it reopened in May 2018 as "Steel Vengeance," when it was described as the world's first hybrid hypercoaster.

"Mean Streak," when it opened at Cedar Point, was both the tallest wooden roller coaster and had the longest drop—at 52 degrees—of any in the world. It operated until 2016, when it was still in the top ten for many aspects of the layout, including lift height, top speed, track-length, and drop distance. It was a Twister model, and construction was mostly of treated southern yellow pine. It closed on September 16, 2016. Rocky Mountain Construction refurbished the ride and opened it as "Steel Vengeance" on May 5, 2018. It now has a 205 ft drop, and broke fifteen records including height (the tallest hybrid), speed (fastest hybrid at 74 mph), length (5,740 ft), and the most airtime on any roller coaster anywhere: 27.2 seconds!

1991: "The Ultimate," Ripon, UK

Status	Operating
Opening date	July 17, 1991
Type	Steel terrain
Manufacturer	British Rail
Designer	Big Country Motioneering/BR Robert Staveley
Lift/launch system	Two chain lift hills
Height	107 ft (33 m)
Length	7,442 ft (2,268 m)
Speed	50 mph (80 km/h)
Duration	7 min 34 sec

Two trains of ten cars. Riders two x two rows: forty riders a train

"The Ultimate," which opened in 1991, is a steel roller coaster at Lightwater Valley amusement park in North Yorkshire, England. When British Rail finished construction—having taken over after the original constructors were sacked— it was 7,442 ft in length, the longest roller coaster in the world, a record which it held for nine years before Steel Dragon 2000 came along for the new millennium. "The Ultimate" is now simply Europe's longest. It needs two (slow) lift hills to make the distance, but as one reviewer put it, it's a roller coaster of two halves: the first smooth and quick, the second, "its evil twin. Like Mr. Hyde to Dr. Jekyll..."

1992: "Batman: The Ride," Gurnee, IL

Status	Operating
Opening date	May 9, 1992
Type	Steel inverted
Manufacturer	Bolliger & Mabillard
Designer	Werner Stengel
Model	Inverted Coaster
Lift/launch system	Chain lift hill
Drop	84.5 ft (26 m)
Length	2,693 or 2,700 ft (821 or 823 m)
Height	100 or 105 ft (30 or 32 m)
Speed	50 mph (80 km/h)
Inversions	Five
Duration	1 min 45 sec
G-force	4 Gs

Trains of eight cars. Riders four x one row: thirty-two riders a train

"Batman: The Ride" is a popular inverted steel roller coaster manufactured by Bolliger & Mabillard that is located at seven different Six Flags Parks across the USA, with clones existing all over the world. The original design was undertaken by Werner Stengel, although Jim Wintrode of Six Flags Great America—the site of the first of the rides to be built—was also involved. This made its debut in 1992, replacing an earlier attraction called "Tidal Wave." The track features five inversions with the top speed experienced being 50 mph (80 km/h). It was the first ride to carry riders below the track and feature inversions.

Right For a short period between May 4, 2013 and July 7, 2013, "Batman: The Ride" ran backwards. This was such a success that other Six Flags "Batman: The Ride" parks followed suit for a limited period in 2014 (Magic Mountain and Texas) and 2015 (Georgia and Great Adventure).

1992: "Vortex,"
Carowinds, Charlotte, NC

Status	Operating
Opening date	March 14, 1992
Type	Steel, stand-up
Manufacturer	Bolliger & Mabillard
Designer	Werner Stengel
Lift/launch system	Chain lift hill
Length	2,040 ft (620 m)
Height	90 ft (27 m)
Speed	50 mph (80 km/h)
Duration	2 min 19 sec

Two trains of six cars. Riders four x one row: twenty-four riders a train

"Vortex" was at the cutting edge of early 1990s stand-up coasters, but now coasters have moved on so much that it is considered a rather tame ride. Riders sit on a bicycle style seat and are secured in place with upper body horse-collar restraints. The run starts with a 90 foot rise up the lift hill, then drops into the first curving loop before soaring up to a large vertical helix, immediately followed by an oblique corkscrew. The ride culminates in a carousel movement before looping through a flat spin and stopping. Stand-up coasters were popular in the 1990s, although now all but five have been replaced in the United States.

1993: "The Outlaw," Altoona, IA

Status	Operating	Height	67 ft (20 m)
Opening date	April 24, 1993	Length	2,800 ft (850 m)
Type	Wood	Speed	48 mph (77 km/h)
Manufacturer	Custom Coasters International	Duration	2 min
Cost	$2 million	One train of six cars. Riders two x two rows: twenty-four riders a train	
Lift/launch system	Chain-lift		

Below Riders experience maximum G-forces of 3.2 and enjoy top speeds of 48 mph on each run of "The Outlaw."

"The Outlaw" is a wooden roller coaster housed in Adventureland, an amusement park that opened in 1974. It opened on April 24, 1993, at a cost of $2 million. Its first significant coaster was the "Tornado"—a large woodie. Success bred success and 1993 saw a major expansion with a Western theme and three rides: "Wrangler," "Chuck Wagon," and "The Outlaw," the latter designed by Mike Boodley who went on to start Great Coasters International. Indeed, "The Outlaw" is considered to be the prototype for later GCI coasters such as "Kentucky Rumbler." With its twister layout and some good airtime, it's the park's most popular ride.

1994: "El Condor," Walibi Holland, Netherlands

Status	Operating
Opening date	May 1994
Type	Steel inverted-suspended looping
Manufacturer	Vekoma
Lift/launch system	Chain lift hill
Height	102 ft (31 m)
Length	2,172 ft (662 m)
Speed	50 mph (80 km/h)
Inversions	Five
Duration	2 min 2 sec
Capacity	900 riders per hour

Two trains of eight cars. Riders two
x one row: sixteen riders a train

"El Condor's" track had turquoise and white
supports until the 2014 season, when they were
repainted orange at the same time as the park in
general was refurbished.

When "El Condor" opened in May 1994 at Walibi Holland in the Netherlands, it was the first in a long line of Vekoma suspended looping roller coasters. A run takes just over two minutes to complete over a track length of 2,172 feet (662 m), during which time riders experience five inversions at speeds of up to 50 mph (80 km/h). The two trains, each of which has eight cars that can carry a total of 16 passengers, rise to a maximum of 102 feet (31 m). Walibi has been through various owners and trials and tribulation, but still has seven coasters and seven thrill rides, as well as a host of family and water rides.

1994: "Raptor," Sandusky, OH

Status	Operating
Opening date	May 7, 1994
Type	Steel inverted
Cost	$11.5–$12 million
Manufacturer	Bolliger & Mabillard
Designer	Werner Stengel
Lift/launch system	Chain lift hill
Drop	119 ft (36 m)
Length	3,790 ft (1,160 m)
Speed	57 mph (92 km/h)
Inversions	Six
Duration	2 min 16 sec

Three trains of eight cars. Riders four x one row: thirty-two riders a train

"Raptor" is a steel inverted roller coaster that broke many records when it first opened at Cedar Point on May 6, 1994. It was the tallest, fastest, and longest, inverted coaster in the world. Werner Stengel's design rises to 137 feet (42 m), and then drops 119 feet (36 m)—but the focus of the layout is on the its inversions, vertical loop, zero-G roll, fearsome cobra roll, and two corkscrews. "Raptor" replaced a ride named "Mill Race" and is as popular as ever, twenty-three years after it opened. In 2017 1,151,349 people flew like a bird of prey. It cost nearly $12 million and most would agree it was worth the money: why else would you stand in line for over two hours for 136 seconds of fun?

"Raptor" mimics the flight of a bird of prey with a 100-foot vertical loop, two inverted corkscrews, a zero gravity roll and the world's first ever cobra roll.

1996: "Big Shot,"
Las Vegas, NV

Status	Operating
Opening date	1996
Type	Space shot
Manufacturer	S&S Worldwide
Designer	Stan Checketts
Height	160 ft (49 m)
Speed	45 mph (72 km/h)
G-force	4 Gs
Duration	35 sec

Riders sit four across: sixteen riders at a time

Left Riders experience 4Gs on the way up and then negative Gs on the way down!

Right Add the skyscraper to the height of the tower and you start from over 1,000 ft up.

"Big Shot" is a pneumatically powered tower ride that is not for those with a fear of heights, being 160 feet (49 m) tall and located on top of the high deck of the 921 feet (281 m) tall Stratosphere skyscraper in Las Vegas. It opened in 1996, and was the highest thrill ride in the world for some time, and still holds the record outside China. This ride, the website suggests, "is not recommended for guests with physical, mental, and/or medical limitations."

1996: "Jurassic Park: The Ride," Hollywood, CA

Universal Studios Hollywood

Status	Operating
Opening date	June 21, 1996

Universal's Islands of Adventure

Status	Operating
Opening date	May 28, 1999

Universal Studios Japan

Status	Operating
Opening date	March 31, 2001

Type	Shoot the Chute
Manufacturer	Vekoma
Designer	Universal Creative
Lift system	Three Chain Lifts
Drop	85 ft (26 m)
Length	1,900 ft (580 m)
Speed	50 mph (80 km/h)
Duration	5 min 30 sec

Riders sit four across x five rows: twenty per ride

There are three versions of this thrill ride designed by Universal Creative and manufactured by Vekoma. Those at the Universal Studios in Hollywood and Japan are both called "Jurassic Park: The Ride," while the third at Universal's Islands of Adventure is labelled "Jurassic Park River Adventure." There was also a similar version built at Universal Studios Singapore which is centered on a rapids ride. The concept was themed on Steven Spielberg's movie *Jurassic Park*, but all that is changing as it is rebranded. The original was a flume-based water ride with great special effects—and a lot of water soaking.

Right This water-based ride closed for nine months in September 2018 to return rebranded into the Jurassic World series.

1996: "Montu," Tampa, FL

"Montu" is an inverted steel roller coaster manufactured by the Swiss Bolliger & Mabillard. It can be found in Busch Gardens: The Dark Continent, an African-themed park that had more than four million visitors in 2015. They come to see the animals and the twenty-plus rides. "Montu" broke a series of records when opened as it immediately became the tallest and fastest inverted coaster in the world. The track has seven inversions, two of which are vertical loops, and non-stop twists and turns. Situated in the Egyptian-themed section of the park, "Montu" is named after the hawk-headed Egyptian god of war.

Status	Operating
Opening date	May 16, 1996
Type	Steel inverted
Cost	$20 million
Manufacturer	Bolliger & Mabillard
Designer	Werner Stengel
Lift/launch system	Chain lift hill
Height	150 ft (46 m)
Drop	128 ft (39 m)
Length	3,983 ft.(1,214 m)
Speed	65 mph (105 km/h)
Inversions	Seven
Duration	3 min
G-force	3.8 Gs

Three trains of eight cars. Riders four x single row: thirty-two riders a train

1997: "Euro-Mir," Rust, Germany

Status	Operating
Opening date	1997
Type	Steel spinning
Manufacturer	Mack Rides
Designer	Franz Mack
Lift/launch system	Spiral Lift
Height	92 ft (28 m)
Length	3,215 ft (980 m)
Speed	49.7 mph (80 km/h)
Duration	4 min 33 sec
G-force	4 Gs

Nine trains of four cars. Riders sit back-to-back two x two rows: sixteen riders a train

Right The ride has a catchy techno soundtrack, dark ride moments and is seriously good, strange fun—"insane" is often used in reviews.

"Euro-Mir" is a steel, spinning roller coaster tin Europa-Park—Germany's largest and Europe's second most popular amusement park with over 5.6 million visitors in 2017. (The most popular? Disneyland Paris, of course.) "Euro-Mir"—one of thirteen rides in the park—is themed around the Russian space station. Riders experience the launch into space and, later, re-entry into Earth's atmosphere. The cars spin at certain times during the ride, the spin tightly controlled by electric motors to ensure the best ride experience.

1997: "Steel Force," Allentown, PA

Status	Operating
Opening date	May 30, 1997
Type	Steel hypercoaster out and back
Cost	$10 million
Manufacturer	D. H. Morgan Manuf.
Designer	Steve Okamoto
Lift/launch system	Chain lift hill
Height	200 ft (61 m)
Drop	205 ft (62 m)
Length	5,600 ft (1,700 m)
Speed	75 mph (121 km/h)
Duration	3 min
G-force	3.4 Gs

Three trains of six cars. Riders two x three rows: thirty-six riders a train

"Steel Force" is one of the best rides on the east coast and is constructed from 2,000 tons of steel, 2,742 anchor bolts, and over 12 million pounds of concrete footers.

"Steel Force" was the tallest, longest, and fastest on the East Coast when it opened in Dorney Park & Wildwater Kingdom in 1997. By that date, Dorney Park had been an attraction for 137 years, having started life in 1860. There are five thrill, seventeen family, three water rides, and seven roller coasters in the park. One of the coasters, "Thunderhawk," dates back to 1923. "Steel Force" dominates the Dorney Park skyline, has a "super first drop" and has stood the test of time to remain one of the top steel rides—and one of the very top for length—around.

1997: "Stampida," Salou, Spain

Status	Operating
Opening date	March 17, 1997
Type	Wooden racing
Manufacturer	Custom Coasters International
Designers	Dennis McNulty, Larry Bill
Lift/launch system	Chain
Height	84 ft (25.6 m)
Length	3,127 ft (953 m)
Speed	46 mph (74.0 km/h)
Duration	1 min 40 sec

Riders two x twelve rows: twenty-four riders a train

"Stampida" is a wooden racing roller coaster at PortAventura Park in Catalonia, Spain. The ride—themed around a dueling wagon train race—opened in 1997. It features a flyby duel, where the trains pass each other in a near head-on collision course. The double track runs parallel at first, then splits apart before rejoining a little later. It has two tunnels and lots of drops. It's an underrated ride, which is overshadowed by "Shambhala" (see p. 39), but is nevertheless, a terrific ride.

The "Stampida" lift hill.

1997: "Superman: Escape from Krypton," Valencia, CA

Status	Operating
Opening date	March 15, 1997
Type	Steel launched shuttle dueling
Cost	$20 million
Manufacturer	Intamin
Lift/launch system	Linear synchronous motor
Height	415 ft (126.5 m)
Drop	328.1 ft (100.0 m)
Length	1,235 ft (376.4 m)
Speed	100 mph (161 km/h)
Duration	28 sec
G-force	4.5 Gs

Cars of four riders x four rows (three in last row): fifteen riders a car

"Superman: Escape from Krypton" (originally called "Superman: The Escape") is a launched-steel dueling shuttle roller coaster located at Six Flags Magic Mountain in California. Opened in 1997 when it was the tallest roller coaster in the world, it provides a stomach turning, fear-inducing, drop that gives 6.5 seconds of weightlessness. Riders are slammed backwards and up at a 90 degree incline and 100 mph for seven seconds—at which point they are weightless for 6.5 seconds—before plummeting at 92 mph back to Earth.

1998: "Riddler's Revenge," Santa Clarita, CA

Status	Operating
Opening date	April 4, 1998
Type	Steel stand-up
Cost	$14 million
Manufacturer	Bolliger & Mabillard
Designer	Werner Stengel
Lift/launch system	Chain lift hill
Height	156 ft (48 m)
Drop	146 ft (45 m)
Length	4,370 ft (1,330 m)
Speed	65 mph (105 km/h)
Inversions	Six
Duration	3 min
G-force	4.2 Gs

Three trains of eight cars. Riders four x single row: thirty-two riders a train

Right Themed for DC Comics' anti-hero the Riddler, (Batman's archenemy), the ride was originally green with black supports, but was changed in 2017 to be green with yellow supports. It sits near "Batman: The Ride."

The "Riddler's Revenge" is a stand-up roller coaster that was designed by Werner Stengel and manufactured by Bolliger & Mabillard, a process that cost $14 million. It opened at Six Flags Magic Mountain on April 4, 1998 at which time it broke records for height (156 ft/48 m), speed (65 mph/105 km/h), drop distance (146 ft/45 m), track length (4,370 ft/ 1,330 m) and the number of inversions—six, that the riders went through. A start to finish run takes three minutes and involves G-forces of up to 4.2.

1998: "Invertigo," Santa Clara, CA

"Invertigo" is an example of a Vekoma shuttle roller coaster, of which four have been built. Modelled on the Boomerang design, it is essentially an inverted version—the example seen here was originally installed at California's Great America under the name "Invertigo," but was later moved to Dorney Park & Wildwater Kingdom in Pennsylvania, whereupon it was renamed "Stinger." A full ride involves two circuits—one forwards, and one backwards—this takes one and a half minutes, during which time passengers experience forces of 5 G.

First manufactured	1997
No. of installations	Four
Manufacturer	Vekoma
Height	131.3 ft (40 m)
Length	1,014 ft (309 m)
Speed	50 mph (80 km/h)
G-Force	5
Duration	1 min 30 sec
Inversions	Three (x2)

One train. Two riders x fourteen rows: twenty-eight riders a train

Operating Installations		
1. "Invertigo"	Kings Island	April 17, 1999
2. "Stinger"	Dorney Park	April 28, 2012
(ex- "Invertigo")	California's Great America	March 21, 1998
3. "Triops"	Bagatelle	June 30, 2012
(ex- "Tornado";	Sommerland Syd	July 2, 2005
Unnamed;	Allou Fun Park	Never opened
ex- "HangOver")	Liseberg	April 1997
4. "Diabolik Invertigo"	Movieland Park	April 24, 2015
(ex- "Two Face: The Flip Side")	Six Flags America	May 8, 1999

Left "Invertigo" is a variation of the traditional Boomerang design by Vekoma.

1998: "Oblivion," Alton Towers, UK

Status	Operating
Opening date	March 14, 1998
Type	Dive
Cost	$20 million
Manufacturer	Bolliger & Mabillard
Designer	Werner Stengel
Lift/launch system	Chain lift hill
Height	65 ft (20 m)
Drop	180 ft (55 m)
Length	1,222 ft (372 m)
Speed	68 mph (109 km/h)
Duration	1 min 11 sec
G-force	4.5 Gs

Seven trains of two cars. Riders eight x single row: sixteen riders a train

"Oblivion" was the world's first dive coaster when it opened, and featured seven trains, each of which carried sixteen riders over its 1,222 feet of track at speeds of up to 68 mph. The seventy-one-second journey isn't long, but there is a stomach-lurching drop of 180 feet into a dark tunnel. One Reviewer said, "The drop is sensational, I count around 3–4 seconds of bliss floaty airtime" then the 4.5 Gs kick in and the ride enters darkness.

Right "Oblivion" is themed to represent a sinister government facility complete with accompanying doom-laden warnings—"Don't Look Down"!

1999: "Dudley Do-Right's Ripsaw Falls," Orlando, FL

Status	Operating
Opening date	May 28, 1999
Type	Flume
Manufacturer	Mack Rides
Height	60 ft (18 m)
Drop	75 ft (23 m)
Speed	45 mph (72 km/h)
Duration	5 min 30 sec

Five riders per boat

"Dudley Do-Right's Ripsaw Falls" is a log flume themed on the Dudley Do-Right of the Mounties cartoon character. It opened on May 28, 1999, on the Universal Islands of Adventure in Florida. As you would expect, this amusement park is full of themed rides from "Skull Island: Reign of Kong," through the Harry Potter-inspired "Flight of the Hippogriff," to Marvel Superhero Island. This ride is in Toon Lagoon and the key element in all the reviews is that it's wet. Very, very wet. There's a dramatic fall of 75 feet (23 m) punctuating the ride and providing the thrills, but most advice says wear your poncho for this great ride.

Left This is a thrill-filled log flume ride that is absolutely guaranteed to soak you!

1999: "Apollo's Chariot," Williamsburg, VA

Status	Operating
Opening date	March 30, 1999
Type	Steel Hyper Coaster
Cost	$20 million
Manufacturer	Bolliger & Mabillard
Designer	Werner Stengel
Lift/launch system	Chain lift hill
Height	170 ft (52 m)
Drop	210 ft (64 m)
Length	4,882 ft (1,488 m)
Speed	73 mph (117 km/h)
Duration	2 min 15 sec
G-force	4.1 Gs

Three trains of nine cars. Riders four x single row: thirty-six riders a train

Left and Above "Apollo's Chariot" is a steel hypercoaster that opened in 1999. It utilizes the existing landscape to sweep smoothly over eight airtime hills with heights ranging between 49 and 131 feet—giving this ride one of the best airtime rides anywhere.

"Apollo's Chariot" is a popular steel hypercoaster that can be found at Busch Gardens Williamsburg, Virginia. Divided into European country areas, "Apollo's Chariot" is in the Italian sector. Hypercoasters are defined as being structures between 200 and 299 feet (60–91 m) high, but this ride still qualifies because although it is only 170 feet (52 m) high, it has a drop of 210 feet (64 m). Regularly rating highly in reviews, with plenty of airtime, "Apollo's Chariot" is one of the best of all steel roller coasters.

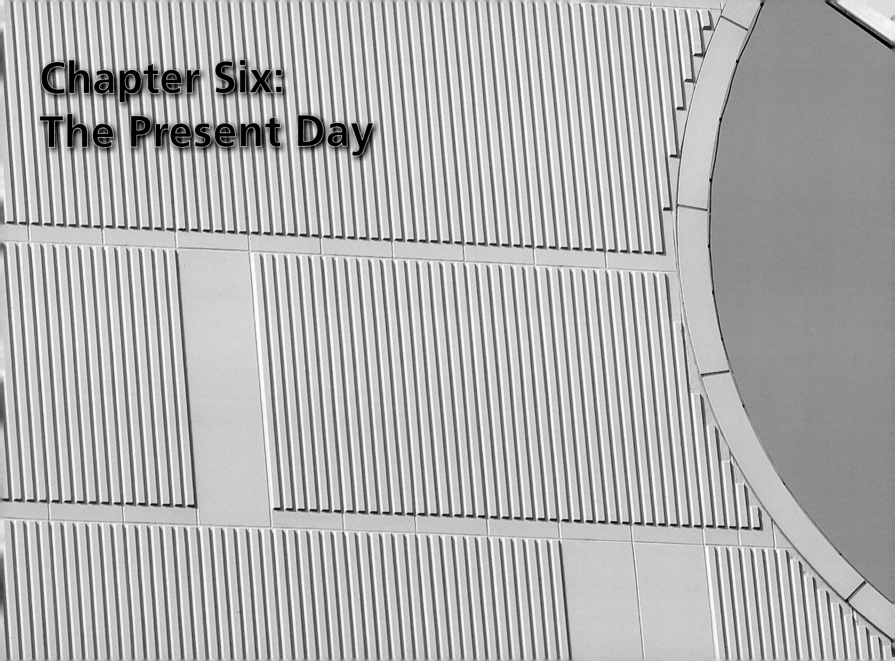

Chapter Six:
The Present Day

2000–2019: AGE OF EXTREME

The start of the new millennium saw thrill ride records fall year on year as the designers pushed the limits of possibility ever further. It began in 2000 when "Millennium Force" at Cedar Point became the first complete-circuit coaster to pass the 300 feet (91 m) tall barrier.

Innovations appeared constantly, including such things as new launch systems, more radical drops, more inversions, and so on.

In 2005, "Kingda Ka" smashed the height records again when it opened—at 456 feet (139 m) into the sky, it had a correspondingly fearsome drop of 418 feet (127 m). Then, the following year, what is considered to be the most expensive ride in the world—"Expedition Everest," opened at Disney's Animal Kingdom. The bar was being set higher and higher!

The 2000s proved beyond doubt that the best way to increase visitor numbers at amusement parks was to offer plenty of new and thrilling rides. This also requires lots of publicity—and in the scramble to establish new records many exciting roller coasters were opened. At the start of the new decade these included "Th13teen" at Alton Towers—which was the first to feature a vertical freefall drop element, and "Formula Rossa" which broke the world speed record for a coaster.

Previous Page "Thunder Dolphin" passes through the La Qua building in the Tokyo Dome City Attractions amusement park. The 3,500 ft (1,067 m) ride reaches 4.4 G and speeds of 81 mph (130 km/h).

Left "Magnum" at Cedar Point Park is definitely not for the faint-hearted!

2000: "Lightning Racer," Hershey, PA

"Lightning Racer" has proved to be particularly popular with riders because the Millennium Flyer trains—built by the same company, are very comfortable to travel in. The track is 3,393 feet long, which takes two minutes twenty seconds to cover. The maximum height being 92 feet, and there is a drop of 90 feet.

Status	Operating
Opening date	May 13, 2000
Type	Wooden racing
Manufacturer	Great Coasters Int.
Lift/launch system	Chain
Height	92 ft (28 m)
Drop	90 ft (27.4 m)
Length	3,393 ft (1,034 m)
Speed	51 mph (82 km/h)
Duration	2 min 20 sec
G-force	3.6 Gs

Four trains of twelve cars. Riders two x single row: twenty-four riders per train

Below "Lightning Racer" is a wooden two track dueling thrill ride—Lightning (red) and Thunder (green). Both rides travel over the same elements but not at the same time.

2000: "Millennium Force," Sandusky, OH

Status	Operating
Opening date	May 13, 2000
Type	Steel gigacoaster out and back
Cost	$25 million
Manufacturer	Intamin
Lift/launch system	Cable lift hill
Height	310 ft (94 m)
Drop	300 ft (91 m)
Length	6,595 ft (2,010 m)
Speed	93 mph (150 km/h)
Duration	2 min 20 sec
G-force	4.5 Gs

Three trains of nine cars. Riders two x two rows: thirty-six riders a train

Right "Millennium Force" was the world's first gigacoaster. After testing, it opened to the public on May 13, 2000 and immediately received rave reviews. It was Cedar Point's most popular ride in 2017—with 1,672,584—and as one commentator put it, "it would not surprise me if it is still #1 after this season, ahead of Steel Vengeance... This is a ride best enjoyed twice." (Craig Webb, Akron Beacon Journal)

"Millennium Force" was the first gigacoaster ever built—at 310 feet (94 m) high, it easily breaks the 300 feet (91 m) threshold for this accolade. It was another winner for Cedar Point amusement park, replacing an earlier ride called "Giant Wheel." It was five years in planning and development. 120 construction workers seven months to build. When it opened in 2000, it immediately established six new world records. These included being the tallest and fastest full circuit coaster. The trains reach a top speed of 93 mph (150 km/h) while navigating the 6,595 feet (2,010 m) long track.

2000: "Steel Dragon 2000," Kuwana, Mie, Japan

Status	Operating
Opening date	August 1, 2000
Type	Steel gigacoaster out and back
Cost	$50 million
Manufacturer	D. H. Morgan Manufacturing
Designer	Steve Okamoto
Lift/launch system	One lift with two chain lifts
Trains built by	Bolliger and Mabillard
Height	318 ft (97 m)
Drop	307 ft (93.5 m)
Length	8,133 ft (2,479 m)
Speed	95 mph (153 km/h)
Duration	4 min

Multiple trains of seven cars. Riders two x two rows: twenty-eight riders a train

"Steel Dragon 2000" is a gigacoaster that was manufactured by Morgan Manufacturing at Nagashima Spa Land amusement park in Mie Prefecture, Japan. As the name suggests, it opened in 2000—which was also the Chinese year of the dragon It was made in Japan and cost an enormous sum to construct, thanks in part to the huge amount of steel required to make it earthquake proof. When built it immediately took the crown of tallest roller coaster in the world, although it didn't hold the accolade for very long. Its track was very long though, and this established a record that stood for many years. The ride suffered a tragic accident in 2003, when a wheel sheared off one of the cars—this caused the coaster to be taken out of service for three years. Since that time, the trains have been completely replaced with ones made by Bolliger and Mabillard.

2000: "Superman the Ride," St. Agawam, MA

Status	Operating
Opening date	May 5, 2000
Type	Steel hypercoaster out and back/twister
Cost	Approx. $12 million
Manufacturer	Intamin
Designer	Werner Stengel
Lift/launch system	Chain lift hill
Height	208 ft (63 m)
Drop	221 ft (67 m)
Length	5,400 ft (1,600 m)
Speed	77 mph (124 km/h)
Duration	2 min 35 sec
G-force	3.6 Gs

Two trains of nine cars. Riders two x two rows: thirty-six riders a train

"Superman the Ride," was originally called "Superman: Ride of Steel," and then "Bizarro," is a steel hypercoaster that was designed by Werner Stengel and manufactured by Intamin at a cost of about $12 million. It opened on May 5, 2000, and is located at Six Flags New England in Agawam, Massachusetts.

The track, which is 5,400 feet (1,600 m) long, is disposed as a combination out and back/twister, having a maximum height of 208 feet (63 m) with a drop of 221 feet (67 m). Riders wear virtual reality masks to ramp the experience up still further and provide extra thrills and excitement.

Right Riders can wear virtual reality head sets so that they can fly along with Superman as he battles Lex Luthor. "Superman the Ride" gives a smooth ride with thrillingly large amounts of airtime and consistently polls at the top of favorite roller coaster experiences.

2000: "Kraken Unleashed," Orlando, FL

"Kraken Unleashed" is a steel floorless roller coaster that was designed by Werner Stengel and manufactured by Bolliger & Mabillard. It is located at SeaWorld Orlando, Florida.

The ride originally opened on June 1, 2000, when it was known simply as "Kraken" (from the mythical sea monster), but this was altered to its current name after a major refit in 2017. The new version saw the introduction of virtual reality headsets for the riders. This provides a whole new experience as they bullet through the seven inversions that include two vertical loops, a dive loop, several rolls, and a spin. Reviews of the experience are mixed, Arthur Levine of *USA Today* said, "VR rides seem not quite ready for prime time. Like the mythical Kraken, they may prove to be elusive"

Status	Operating
Opening date	June 1, 2000 (as "Kraken") June 16, 2017 (as "Unleashed")
Type	Floorless
Manufacturer	Bolliger & Mabillard
Designer	Werner Stengel
Lift/launch system	Chain lift hill
Height	153 ft (47 m)
Drop	144 ft (44 m)
Length	4,177 ft (1,273 m)
Speed	65 mph (105 km/h)
Inversions	seven
Duration	2 min 2 sec
G-force	3.9 Gs

Three trains of eight cars. Riders four x one row: thirty-two riders a train

2000: "Goliath," Los Angeles, CA

"Goliath" is a steel hypercoaster that was designed by Werner Stengel and manufactured by Giovanola of Switzerland which cost $30 million to construct. It is located at Six Flags Magic Mountain in Valencia, California, where it is laid out through sub-tropical scenery that depicts the ruins of the ancient Mayan civilization.

"Goliath" is a twister format coaster that opened on February 11, 2000 and briefly held the titles of longest and fastest drop in the world, before losing them to a rival ride.

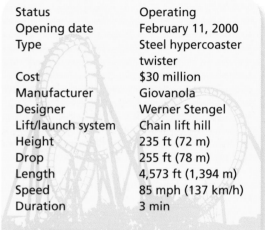

Status	Operating
Opening date	February 11, 2000
Type	Steel hypercoaster twister
Cost	$30 million
Manufacturer	Giovanola
Designer	Werner Stengel
Lift/launch system	Chain lift hill
Height	235 ft (72 m)
Drop	255 ft (78 m)
Length	4,573 ft (1,394 m)
Speed	85 mph (137 km/h)
Duration	3 min

Three trains of five cars. Riders two x three rows: thirty riders a train

Left After cresting the first hill "Goliath" plunges 255 feet down into the dirt and through a dark underground tunnel, and then drops an even further 185 feet. The second half of the ride twists and turns, pulling over 4.5 Gs, providing a really intense, thrilling adventure.

2001: "Hypersonic XLC," Doswell, VA

Status	Removed
Opening date	March 24, 2001
Closing date	October 28, 2007
Type	Steel launched out and back
Cost	$15 million
Manufacturer	S&S Worldwide
Designer	S&S Worldwide
Lift/launch system	Pneumatic
Height	165 ft (50 m)
Drop	133 ft (41 m)
Length	1,560 ft (480 m)
Speed	80 mph (130 km/h)
Duration	16 seconds
G-force	4.0 Gs

Trains of four cars. Riders two x one row: eight riders per train

"Hypersonic XLC" was a roller coaster that was manufactured by S&S Worldwide and originally sited in Utah. Since then it has been relocated to Kings Dominion in Doswell, Virginia. At this stage, various modifications were made to make it fit the differently-shaped terrain of its new home as well as to improve the ride.

Opening on March 24, 2001, "Hypersonic XLC" was the first compressed-air-launched coaster in the world. After experiencing all manner of technical problems, it was closed on October 28, 2007 before being dismantled.

Left and Right "Hypersonic XLC" accelerated from a standstill to 80 mph in 1.8 seconds. When it closed in 2007 it was dismantled, stored, and put up for sale but there were no takers. It is rumored that it has been scrapped and recycled.

2001: "Do-Dodonpa,"
Fujiyoshida, Japan

Status	Operating
Opening date	November 21, 2001
Type	Steel air-launched
Manufacturer	S&S Worldwide
Lift/launch system	Compressed air
Height	161 ft (49 m)
Length	4,081 ft (1,244 m)
Speed	110 mph (180 km/h)
Inversions	One
Duration	55 sec
G-force	4.25 Gs

Four trains of four cars. Riders two x one row: eight riders per train

Right After "Do-Dodonpa" was refurbished in 2016, it came back even faster in 2017, reaching 119 mph. It has four trains painted with different faces—father, mother, brother, and sister.

"Do-Dodonpa" is an compressed air-launched steel roller coaster that was built by S&S Worldwide and opened on December 21, 2001. Originally called simply "Dodonpa," it is located at Fuji-Q Highland in Fujiyoshida, Yamanashi, Japan. On its inauguration it took two world records—with its cars going from 0 to 110 mph (180 km/h) in 1.56 seconds, it was the fastest accelerating coaster in existence—the top speed also meant that it was the fastest too. With a duration of only 55 seconds, the ride isn't particularly long, but that is mostly because it is covered at such a high speed! The 2016–2017 revamp saw the so-called "top hat" (like "Hypersonic XLC") replaced by the largest vertical loop in the world—130 ft 3 in (39.7 m) in diameter—visible in the photo at left. It has remarkable acceleration—it reaches 110 mph some 1.5 seconds after firing—but has had mixed reviews. It's so extreme it hurts.

2001: "Nitro," Jackson, NJ

Status	Operating
Opening date	April 7, 2001
Type	Steel hypercoaster
Cost	$20 million
Manufacturer	Bolliger & Mabillard
Track layout	L-shaped Out and Back
Lift/launch system	Chain lift hill
Height	230 ft (70 m)
Drop	215 ft (66 m)
Length	5,394 ft (1,644 m)
Speed	80 mph (130 km/h)
Duration	2 min 20 sec
G-force	4.3 Gs

Three trains of nine cars. Riders four x one row: thirty-six riders a train

The colorful track is pink and yellow with blue supports. It has a top speed of 80 mph and a ride time of 2 minutes and 20 seconds that includes an intense G-force inducing double helix element.

"Nitro" is a steel out and back hypercoaster that was designed by Bolliger & Mabillard with the fabrication work being undertaken by Clermont Steel Fabricators of Batavia, Ohio. It cost Six Flags Great Adventure in Jackson, New Jersey, $20 million to build and install. When it opened on April 7, 2001, it was both the fastest and the tallest in that part of the country.

"Nitro" pulls big trains with thirty-six passengers and is, quite simply, one of the top thrill rides in the world combining height, speed, and airtime.

2002: "Wicked Twister,"
Cedar Point, Sandusky, OH

Status	Operating
Opening date	May 5, 2002
Type	Inverted impulse steel coaster
Manufacturer	Intamin
Designer	Werner Stengel
Cost	$9,000,000
Lift/launch system	LIM launch track
Height	215 ft (66 m)
Length	675 ft (206 m)
Speed	72 mph (116 km/h)
Duration	0.40
G-force	2.1

One train of eight cars. Riders two x two: 32 riders per train

Riders submit themselves to a thrilling back and forth ride between two tall spiky towers that twist vertically around 450 degrees. They are joined at the base by a horizontal track where the linear induction motor propulsion system and the platform where passengers get on and off is located.

The ride bursts out onto the teal and sunburst yellow tracks at 50 mph and shoots about halfway up the front tower, it halts and then falls. Now it shoots backwards and climbs halfway up the second tower. It stops and drops again and then relaunches moving right to the top of the first tower. It stops and reverses again, and is re-launched right to the top of the rear tower. It drops again and powers up the first tower before dropping back to the station platform and disembarkation.

2002: "Xcelerator," Buena Park, CA

Status	Operating
Opening date	June 22, 2002
Type	Steel launched dual overbank figure of eight
Cost	$25 million
Manufacturer	Intamin
Designer	Werner Stengel
Lift/launch system	Hydraulic catch car
Height	205 ft (62 m)
Length	2,202 ft (671 m)
Speed	82 mph (132 km/h)
Duration	1 min 2 sec

Two trains of five cars. Riders two x two rows: twenty riders a train

With cars themed to look like chrome-plated and fin-tailed '57 Chevvies, this ride recalls all the retro excitement of 50s-era teenage racing. "Xcelerator" at Knott's Berry Farm replaces an earlier ride called "Windjammer Surf Racers." It was the company's first ride to use a hydraulic catapult to launch a train—the twin motors each develop 10,500 hp (7,800 kW) while doing so. As a result of this thrust, the train accelerates from rest to 82 mph (132 km/h) in 2.3 seconds in only 157 feet (48 m). The motors are actually powerful enough to achieve far more than this—but are carefully limited for reasons of public safety.

2002: "Colossus," Thorpe Park, UK

Status	Operating	Drop	97 ft (30 m)
Opening date	March 22, 2002	Length	2,789 ft (850 m)
Type	Steel multi-inversion	Speed	45 mph (72 km/h)
Track layout	Intamin Tri Track	Inversions	Ten
Cost	£13.5 million	Duration	1 min 45 sec
Manufacturer	Intamin	G-force	4.2 Gs
Designer	Werner Stengel		
Lift/launch system	Chain lift hill	Two trains of seven cars. Riders two x two	
Height	98 ft (30 m)	rows: twenty-eight riders a train	

"Colossus" is a steel multi-inversion roller coaster. Riders are treated to G-forces of up to 4.2 on this multi-inversion (ten!) thrill ride. It is loosely themed around Ancient Greece and the long lost city of Atlantis. To explore, riders pass through a vertical loop, a cobra roll, two corkscrews, and five heartline rolls.

2003: "Top Thrill Dragster," Sandusky, OH

"Top Thrill Dragster" is a hydraulically launched, steel stratacoaster that was designed by Werner Stengel and built by Intamin for Cedar Point in Sandusky, Ohio, at a cost of $25 million. Opening in May 2003, it is a staggering 420 feet (130 m) tall, with an intimidating drop of 400 feet (120 m). The track is 2,800 feet (850 m) long, and the trains are accelerated from rest to a top speed of 120 mph (190 km/h) in 3.8 seconds. It replaced earlier rides called "Chaos," and "Troika."

Status	Operating
Opening date	May 4, 2003
Type	Steel accelerator
Cost	$25 million
Manufacturer	Intamin
Designer	Werner Stengel
Lift/launch system	Hydraulic Launch
Height	420 ft (130 m)
Drop	400 ft (120 m)
Length	2,800 ft (850 m)
Speed	120 mph (190 km/h)
Duration	30 sec
Acceleration	0 to 120 mph in 3.8 sec

Six trains of five cars. Riders two x two rows (except for first car): eighteen riders a train

Left Because of the extreme nature of the design, "Top Thrill Dragster" is very sensitive to strong winds and any precipitation at all. In these circumstances the ride is canceled until weather conditions improve. Very occasionally the ride doesn't have enough speed to crest the top, in which case it can roll back—but this is halted by magnetic brakes.

2004: "Thunderhead," Pigeon Forge, TN

Dollywood is Tennessee's biggest draw and sees over two million visitors, who consistently give it high rankings—*USA Today*'s readers rated it sixth best in the United States. There are forty rides, including eight roller coasters, of which "Thunderhead" is a Great Coasters International woodie that took 700,000 feet of Southern Yellow pine boards to construct. It must have been a difficult build because this is an amazingly complex construction that delivers a great ride, with twenty-two turns, thirty-two crossovers, and a station fly through that also builds anticipation in the waiting crowds.

Status	Operating
Opening date	April 3, 2004
Type	Wooden twister
Cost	$7 million
Manufacturer	Great Coasters International
Designer	Mike Boodley
Lift/launch system	Chain lift hill
Height	100.4 ft (30.6 m)
Drop	100 ft (30 m)
Length	3,230 ft (980 m)
Speed	53.7 mph (86.4 km/h)
Inversions	None
Duration	2 min 30 sec
Max vertical angle	60 degrees

Twelve cars. Riders two x one row; twenty-four riders a train

2005: "Kingda Ka," Jackson Township, NJ

The hydraulic launch system rockets the train to 128 mph in 3.5 seconds: the entire ride usually takes well less than a minute, depending on weather conditions, the weight of the passengers, and other variables—and it's regularly voted the scariest ride on the planet.

Status	Operating
Opening date	May 21, 2005
Type	Steel accelerator stratacoaster
Manufacturer	Intamin
Designer	Werner Stengel
Lift/launch system	Hydraulic launch
Height	456 ft (139 m)
Drop	418 ft (127 m)
Length	3,118 ft (950 m)
Speed	128 mph (206 km/h)
Duration	59 sec
G-force	5 Gs

Four trains of five cars. Riders two x two rows (except for last car): eighteen riders a train

"Kingda Ka" is an infamous steel accelerator stratacoaster coaster—only the second stratacoaster ever built—and immediately established a new world record for the tallest and fastest coaster. It is located at Six Flags Great Adventure in Jackson, New Jersey, and has almost the same layout as "Top Thrill Dragster" in Ohio. What's it like to ride? Boosted up the ninety-degree top hat tower, the train then returns to earth via a 270-degree vertical spiral. "It's hard to imagine anything more thrilling," said one reviewer; "insane acceleration" said another. That about sums it up.

2006: "Goliath," Austell, GA

Status	Operating
Opening date	April 1, 2006
Type	Steel out and back
Cost	$20 million
Manufacturer	Bolliger & Mabillard
Model	Hypercoaster
Lift/launch system	Chain lift hill
Height	200 ft (61 m)
Drop	175 ft (53 m)
Length	4,480 ft (1,370 m)
Speed	70 mph (110 km/h)
Duration	3 min 30 sec

Two trains of nine cars. Riders four x one row: thirty-six riders a train

Not to be confused with the tallest woodie in the world at sister park Six Flags Great America, this "Goliath" is a steel out and back hypercoaster located at Six Flags Over Georgia. "Goliath" replaced earlier rides "Great Gasp" and "Looping Starship." And it's a winner! Tall, fast, with plenty of airtime and a great downward helix, "Goliath" is the best coaster in the park: intense, undoubtedly, but smooth and in most riders' top ten steel coasters.

2006: "Eejanaika," Yamanashi, Japan

Status	Operating
Opening date	July 19, 2006
Type	Steel Fourth dimension
Cost	$31 million
Manufacturer	S&S Arrow
Model	Fourth dimension
Lift/launch system	Chain lift hill
Height	249.33 ft (76 m)
Length	3,783 ft (1,153 m)
Speed	78.3 mph (126.0 km/h)
Inversions	Three, + 11 seat inversions

Trains of five cars. Riders four x one row: twenty riders a train

Above "Eejanaika" gives riders three types of spins, "the spinning of your seat forward and backward," "loops and flip-flops through the air," and "spinning with twists in it"—all at 78 mph.

"Eejanaika" means "Ain't it Great" and most people wold agree that this steel fourth-dimension roller hypercoaster is just that. It's located in Fuji-Q Highland along with forty or so rides, including a number of high-quality extreme rides. "Eejanaika" opened in 2006, and the riders of this 4th-dimension coaster undergo fourteen inversions, equaling those of "The Smiler" at Alton Towers, UK. However, only three of the inversions are actually due to the track. The others are all performed by spinning the seats, a feat that is controlled by two extra rails which interact with a rack and pinion gear set.

2006: "El Toro," Jackson, NJ

"El Toro" is a wooden out and back roller coaster that was designed by Werner Stengel and manufactured by Intamin in conjunction with Rocky Mountain Construction. The name is Spanish for "The Bull," and the ride is located at Six Flags Great Adventure in Jackson, New Jersey. It replaced the previous ride called "Viper."

When it opened on June 12, 2006, its statistics put it firmly on the world scene. With a 176 feet (54 m) drop that was inclined at 76 degrees, it was the steepest of any wooden roller coaster in existence, as well as being the second highest. It also broke new ground in that the cable lift was a first for a wooden ride.

Status	Operating
Opening date	June 12, 2006
Type	Wooden out and back
Cost	$25 million
Manufacturer	Intamin
Designer	Werner Stengel
Lift/launch system	Cable lift hill
Height	181 ft (55 m)
Drop	176 ft (54 m)
Length	4,400 ft (1,300 m)
Speed	70 mph (110 km/h)
Duration	1 min 42 sec
G-force	4.4 Gs

Two trains of six cars. Riders two x three rows: thirty-six riders a train

Left "El Toro" is a twisting, turning ride that simulates the bucking and tossing of a bull. It is a wonderfully fast and smooth ride with nine air time experiences. It regularly tops popularity lists of best wooden thrill rides.

2008: "T Express," Yongin, South Korea

Status	Operating
Opening date	March 14, 2008
Type	Wooden terrain
Manufacturer	Intamin
Designer	Werner Stengel
Lift/launch system	Cable lift
Height	184 ft (56 m)
Drop	151 ft (46 m)
Length	5,384 ft (1,641 m)
Speed	65 mph (104 km/h)

Three trains of six cars. Riders two x three rows: thirty-six riders a train

"T Express" is a Werner Stengel-designed wooden roller coaster that was manufactured by Intamin with assistance from Rocky Mountain Construction. "T Express" exploits the natural topography to obtain the best possible ride experience. This gives it a maximum height of 184 feet, a drop of 151 feet, and speeds of 65 mph. Opening on March 14, 2008, at Everland Resort in Yongin, South Korea, it utilizes a cable lift for the launch and featured highly in the world rankings for its height, length, and speed. It is one of five roller coasters on the site, which received 6.31 million visitors in 2017—down from a maximum of 7.42 million visitors in 2015.

2008: "Fahrenheit," Hershey, PA

Status	Operating
Opening date	May 24, 2008
Type	Steel vertical lift
Cost	$12 million
Manufacturer	Intamin
Lift/launch system	Vertical chain lift
Height	121 ft (37 m)
Length	2,700 ft (820 m)
Speed	58 mph (93 km/h)
Inversions	Six
Duration	1 min 25 sec

Three trains of three cars. Riders
two x two rows: twelve riders a train

"Fahrenheit" is a steel vertical lift roller coaster that was announced in a press release at the end of the 2007 season, before opening the following year on May 24, 2008. It was built with six inversions by Intamin at a cost of around $12 million, and is located at Hersheypark in Hershey, Pennsylvania.

On its inauguration, "Fahrenheit" took the world record for being the steepest roller coaster—due to its maximum angle of 97 degrees— although it has since slid down the rankings a little due to the opening of newer models. It is one of only three roller coasters in the world to feature a Norwegian loop (a type of double inversion).

2009: "Blue Fire,"
Rust, Germany

Status	Operating
Opening date	April 4 2009
Type	Steel launched full-circuit dark ride
Manufacturer	Mack Rides
Lift/launch system	LSM-launched lift hill
Height	124 ft (38 m)
Length	3,464 ft (1,056 m)
Speed	62 mph (100 km/h)
Inversions	Four
Duration	2 min 30 sec
G-force	3.8 Gs

Five trains of five cars. Riders two x two rows: twenty riders a train

"Blue Fire" is a steel roller coaster located at Europa-Park in Germany—often nominated the best theme park in Europe—and its name comes from its natural gas company sponsor. It begins as a dark ride and then turns into a launched coaster. The first part lasts around 45 seconds, and then the rest—when the train accelerates to 62 mph in 2.5 seconds—adds a further 1 min 45 sec to the ride, including passing through four inversions and decent landscaping—as themeparkinsider.com puts it, "This ain't no roller coaster in a parking lot."

"Saw–The Ride" is another example of a part-enclosed dark ride, part daylight experience. Photo shows the free-fall drop and some well-placed blades.

2009: "Saw–The Ride,"
Thorpe Park, UK

Status	Operating
Opening date	March 14, 2009
Type	Steel Euro-fighter
Cost	£13.5 million
Manufacturer	Gerstlauer
Designer	Merlin Studios
Track layout	Custom
Lift/launch system	Vertical chain lift hill
Height	100 ft (30 m)
Length	2,362 ft (720 m)
Speed	55 mph (89 km/h)
Inversions	Three
Duration	1 min 40 sec
G-force	4.7 Gs

Eight trains of one car. Riders four x two rows: eight riders a train

A one-time gravel pit, Thorpe Park opened in 1979 and has twenty-nine rides with seven roller coasters, including the highly rated "The Swarm" set in London during an alien attack, and "Stealth" which is fast and furious. None of the rides, however, eclipses "Saw–The Ride," a Merlin Studios-designed steel Euro-fighter ride that sells itself as "the world's first horror movie roller coaster." It was the first ever to feature a 100-degree free-fall drop, although this figure has since been surpassed by newer coasters. The vertical lift hill and the dark start lead to a lot of nerves and the occasional "essential cleaning."

2010: "Formula Rossa," Abu Dhabi, UAE

Status	Operating
Opening date	November 4, 2010
Type	Steel launched
Manufacturer	Intamin
Designer	Jack Rouse Associates
Lift/launch system	Hydraulic
Height	171 ft (52 m.)
Drop	169 ft (51.5 m)
Length	6,790 ft (2,070 m)
Speed	150 mph (240 km/h)
Duration	1 min 32 sec
G-force	4.8 Gs

Four trains of four cars. Riders two x two rows: sixteen riders a train

"Formula Rossa" is a roller coaster that has a definite emphasis on speed—it uses a hydraulic launch system to accelerate the trains from rest to 150 mph (240 km/h) in four seconds, with 62 mph (100 km/h) being reached in just two seconds! This makes it the fastest roller coaster in the world.

Located at Ferrari World in Abu Dhabi, United Arab Emirates, as its name suggests, the theme park celebrates Ferrari's past and future. The closest you can get to racing an F1 Ferrari, riders are given eyewear to protect from the wind caused by the 20,800 hp launch. The ride has an impressively long track, but still only last ninety seconds or so.

2010: "Th13teen," Alton Towers, UK

Status	Operating
Opening date	March 20, 2010
Cost	£15 million
Type	Steel family drop
Manufacturer	Intamin
Designer	John Wardly
Lift/launch system	Drive tire lift hill
Height	65.6 ft (20 m)
Drop	60 ft (18 m)
Length	2,480 ft (760 m)
Speed	42 mph (68 km/h)
G-force	3.2 Gs

Trains of five cars. Riders two x two rows: twenty riders a train

"Th13teen" is categorized as a dark ride and pre-launch PR dubbed it "the scariest roller coaster in the world." When it opened in 2010, it replaced the iconic 1980—and much-loved—ride called "Corkscrew," which introduced the double helix. "Th13teen" had a lot to live up to and delivered the world's first vertical freefall drop element—when a horizontal section of track on which the train halts actually freefalls downwards—a maneuver undertaken in complete darkness. This certainly helped draw in the crowds and Alton Towers benefited with attendances up around 2.5 million. (They dropped substantially in 2015 following the awful accident on "The Smiler," but are improving again now.)

Below and Right The outdoor section of "Th13teen" is fast and smooth.

2011: "Raptor," Castelnuovo del Garda, Italy

Status	Operating
Opening date	April 1, 2011
Cost	$14 million
Type	Steel wing twister
Manufacturer	Bolliger & Mabillard
Lift/launch system	Chain lift hill
Height	108.3 ft (33 m)
Length	2,526.3 ft (770 m)
Speed	56 mph (90 km/h)
Inversions	Three
Duration	1 min and 30 sec

Two trains of seven cars. Riders four x single row: twenty-eight riders a train

"Raptor" features three different inversions: a corkscrew, a zero-g roll, and an inline twist.

This steel wing coaster is laid out as a twister at the Gardaland amusement park, Italy's best theme park, opened in 1975. (It's well attended, too: the 2017 European Top 20 had it eighth, with over 2.6 million visitors. Forbes has it fifth in the world by turnover.) Part of the appeal of the park is the selection of roller coasters—seven of them including "Raptor," which opened in 2011 in place of "Tunga the Apeman." Designed as a prototype, "Raptor" includes two watersplash elements—riders get soaked!—and several inversions, and was Italy's first wing coaster. It's well-themed has plenty of atmosphere with at least six headchopper near misses, and seems to be aging well.

2011: "New Texas Giant," Arlington, TX

The "New Texas Giant" started out as a wooden roller coaster simply known as the "Texas Giant," but after many years it had deteriorated to the point that it had become distinctly uncomfortable. As a result, this once-popular ride was withdrawn from service. Rather than dismantle it though, Six Flags Over Texas brought in Rocky Mountain Construction to give the structure a complete refurbishment. During this process, the track was replaced with steel and a host of other improvements were made before it was reopened in 2011 under its new name—"New Texas Giant."

Status	Operating
Opening date	April 22, 2011
Type	I-Box
Cost	$10 million
Manufacturer	Rocky Mountain Construction
Designer	Alan Schilke
Lift/launch system	Chain lift hill
Height	153 ft (47 m)
Drop	147 ft (45 m)
Length	4,200 ft (1,300 m)
Speed	65 mph (105 km/h)
Duration	3 min 25 sec
G-force	4.2 Gs

Three trains of six cars. Riders two x two rows: twenty-four riders a train

The cars are manufactured by Gerstlauer and designed to resemble 1961 Cadillac Devilles, complete with chrome grills and horn hood ornaments on the lead cars. It runs on bright orange IBox track that give a really smooth ride.

2011: "Takabisha," Yamanashi, Japan

Status	Operating	Length	3,300 ft (1,000 m)
Opening date	July 16, 2011	Speed	62 mph (100 km/h)
Type	Steel launched Euro-fighter	Inversions	Seven
		Duration	2 min 40 sec
Cost	$28.5 million	G-force	4.6 Gs
Manufacturer	Gerstlauer		
Lift/launch system	LIM, chain lift hill	Six cars. Riders four x two rows: eight riders per car	
Height	141 ft (43 m)		

Another exciting ride in Fufi-Q Highland, "Takabisha" has the steepest drop angle —121 degrees—of any coaster in the world. Opened in 2011, it features a linear induction motor launch as well as a chain lift hill. Although at a maximum of 141 feet it is not particularly high, it does have seven inversions to go with its fearsome drop. "Takabisha" hits 62 mph in two seconds and means "Domineering" in Japanese.

"Takabisha" —at the extreme right of the photo is the tower and the 121-degree drop.

2012: "Leviathan," Vaughan, Canada

"Leviathan," at 306 feet (93 m) high, was the first by the Swiss manufacturer to break into the gigacoaster category. It is located at Canada's Wonderland and is Canada's tallest and fastest roller coaster. Opened in 1981, Canada's Wonderland has sixty-nine rides, including sixteen coasters, and in 2017 had over 3.75 million visitors. With a lift hill that goes on forever, an 80-degree first drop, plenty of airtime

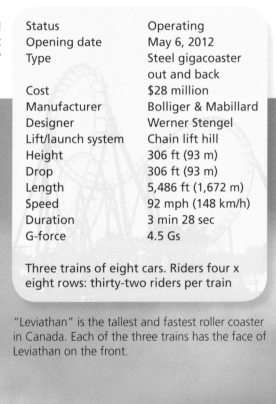

Status	Operating
Opening date	May 6, 2012
Type	Steel gigacoaster out and back
Cost	$28 million
Manufacturer	Bolliger & Mabillard
Designer	Werner Stengel
Lift/launch system	Chain lift hill
Height	306 ft (93 m)
Drop	306 ft (93 m)
Length	5,486 ft (1,672 m)
Speed	92 mph (148 km/h)
Duration	3 min 28 sec
G-force	4.5 Gs

Three trains of eight cars. Riders four x eight rows: thirty-two riders per train

"Leviathan" is the tallest and fastest roller coaster in Canada. Each of the three trains has the face of Leviathan on the front.

2013: "Ring Racer," Nürburg, Germany

Status	Closed
Opening date	October 31, 2013
Closing date	November 4, 2013
Type	Steel launched
Cost	$13.5 million
Track layout	Racetrack oval
Manufacturer	S&S Worldwide
Lift/launch system	Pneumatic launch
Height	123 ft (37.5 m)
Length	3,976 ft (1,212 m)
Speed	99.4 mph (160 km/h)
Duration	85 sec
G-force	5.6 Gs

Two trains of two cars. Riders two x two rows: eight riders a train

Built as part of the Nürburgring 2009 development, which collapsed at great loss to the Rheinland-Pfalz taxpayers, "Ring Racer" is closed but still standing.

"Ring Racer" is/was a steel launched roller coaster with a Formula One theme that should have opened on August 15, 2009, at the Nürburgring motor racing circuit. Technical problems, however—including several explosions in the pneumatic launch system— meant that it didn't actually do so until 2013.

The original plan was for the trains to accelerate from rest to 135 mph (217 km/h) in 2.5 seconds, but this proved impractical. It was finally configured to achieve 100 mph (160 km/h) in under 2 seconds, but even then the S&S Worldwide ride proved to be uneconomic to run and it was closed within a few days.

2013: "GateKeeper," Sandusky, OH

Status	Operating
Opening date	May 11, 2013
Type	Steel wing out and back
Cost	$30 million
Manufacturer	Bolliger & Mabillard
Lift/launch system	Chain lift hill
Height	170 ft (52 m)
Drop	164 ft (50 m)
Length	4,164 ft (1,269 m)
Speed	67 mph (108 km/h)
Inversions	Six
Duration	2 min 40 sec
G-force	4 Gs

Three trains of eight cars. Riders four x one row: thirty-two riders a train

"GateKeeper" features a chain lift hill and holds the world record for its 170 feet (52 m) high inversion. It took almost 100 workers, from four engineering companies, over eight months to construct "GateKeeper." It also broke records for its top speed, track length (4,164 ft/1,269 m), drop height (164 ft/50 m), as well as for having six inversions. The first ride you see at Cedar Point's front gate, "GateKeeper" proved its second most popular ride in 2017, with 1,588,646 passengers. It replaced the earlier rides "Disaster Transport," and "Space Spiral."

2013: "Outlaw Run," Branson, MO

Status	Operating
Opening date	March 15, 2013
Type	Wooden terrain
Cost	$10 million
Manufacturer	Rocky Mountain Construction
Designer	Alan Schilke
Lift/launch system	Chain lift hill
Height	107 ft (33 m)
Drop	162 ft (49 m)
Length	2,937 ft (895 m)
Speed	68 mph (109 km/h)
Inversions	Three
Duration	1 min 27 sec

Two trains of six cars. Riders two x two rows: twenty-four riders a train

"Outlaw Run" is a wooden roller coaster at the Silver Dollar City park in Branson, Missouri. Themed on a Western stagecoach, the ride has to avoid outlaws intent on stealing the mail and robbing the passengers. Designed by Alan Schilke and manufactured by Rocky Mountain Construction for $10 million, it was the first wooden coaster to feature three inversions on its track, which is covered at speeds of up to 68 mph (109km/h).

2013: "The Smiler," Alton Towers, UK

The coaster had some teething problems but its 14 inversions make it a hard act to beat.

Status	Operating
Opening date	May 31, 2013
Type	Steel infinity (or dive)
Cost	£18 million
Manufacturer	Gerstlauer
Track layout	Infinity Coaster 1170
Lift/launch system	Two chain lift systems
Drop	98.4 ft (30 m)
Length	3,838.6 ft (1,170 m)
Speed	52.8 mph (85.0 km/h)
Inversions	Fourteen
Duration	2 min 45 sec
G-force	4.5 Gs

Four trains of four cars. Riders four x single row: sixteen riders a train

"The Smiler" is a steel infinity roller coaster that opened on May 31, 2013, replacing a ride called "The Black Hole." It broke new ground with its stomach-turning fourteen (!) inversions, establishing a new world record. With a 3D lightshow to keep the waiting punters amused—as do the glimpses of the ride careening overhead—it ticked every box. It's had a checkered career: a delay in the opening by two months and a major accident in in 2015 and since that date the park has struggled to rebuild its attendance figures.

2013: "Full Throttle," Valencia, CA

Status	Operating
Opening date	June 22, 2013
Type	Steel launched Terrain
Cost	$6 million
Manufacturer	Premier Rides
Lift/launch system	Three linear synchronous motors
Height	160 ft (49 m)
Length	2,200 ft (670 m)
Speed	70 mph (110 km/h)
Inversions	Two
Duration	1 min 30 sec
G-force	4.0 Gs

Two trains of three cars. Riders two x three rows: eighteen riders a train

"Full Throttle" is located at the Six Flags Magic Mountain amusement park. It replaced "Log Jammer," and at the time of its inauguration, its 160-feet high vertical loop was the tallest in the world. "Full Throttle" boasts of having the highest, fastest, and first-ever top-hat loop—so riders can fly across the inside and outer rail of the circle. The launch system uses three linear synchronous motors, although only one at a time, and the three separate launches mean that the ride is a continual surprise. First launch gets you going on the inside of the loop; second launch is backwards; the third powers the train round the outside and back to the station. Fantastic!

2014: "Falcon's Fury," Tampa, FL

"Falcon's Fury" allows riders to experience a fantastic view of downtown Tampa and the Busch Gardens resort as the car is lifted to the top of the tower. Then it tilts riders 90 degrees and holds for a random time of one to five seconds—the latter feeling like an eternity—before, uniquely, dropping them face first downwards. After about five seconds of free fall, the riders reach a speed of around 60 mph—channeling their inner falcon and dropping like a predator down the tallest free-standing drop tower in North America. After a couple of seconds the magnetic brakes kick in and soon after, the hydraulic pistons bring the riders back up "Falcon's Fury" replaced "Sandstorm," and was manufactured by a subsidiary of Intamin—Intaride—along with 6,000 bolts, and although it wasn't ready on time, issing the summer 2014 crowds, it's delivered ever since. It's tall and terrifying, and rather addictive.

Status	Operating
Opening date	September 2, 2014
Type	Drop tower
Cost	$5–6 million
Manufacturer	Intamin
Height	335 ft (102 m)
Drop	310 ft (94 m)
Speed	60 mph (97 km/h)
G-force	3.5 Gs
Duration	2 min

One car: Riders four x one row: thirty-two in total

2014: "Goliath," Six Flags Great America, Gurnee, IL

Status	Operating
Opening date	June 19, 2014
Type	Custom Topper Track
Manufacturer	Rocky Mountain Construction
Designer	Alan Schilke
Lift/launch system	Chain lift hills
Height	165 ft (50 m)
Length	3,100 ft (940 m)
Speed	72 mph (116 km/h)
Duration	1 min 45 sec

Two trains of six cars. Riders two x two rows: 24 riders per train

When it opened "Goliath" immediately took three wooden roller coaster records—the fastest speed at 72 mph (116 km/h), the longest drop on a roller coaster of 180 ft (55 m), and the steepest drop at a stomach-losing 85 degrees. To make the ride even more exciting, it incorporates two tunnels, a dive loop, zero-G stalls, two inversions, and two over-banked curves.

The track is known as Topper Track and is made up of six layers of laminated wood topped with steel square tubing that is the actual track. This was specially designed to provide a smoother ride and to reduce the typically high maintenance required by woodies.

2015: "Twisted Colossus," Santa Clarita, CA

Status	Operating
Opening date	May 23, 2015
Type	Steel I-Box
Cost	$7 million
Manufacturer	Rocky Mountain Construction
Designer	Alan Schilke
Track layout	Möbius Loop
Lift/launch system	Chain lift hill
Height	121 ft (37 m)
Drop	128 ft (39 m)
Length	4,990 ft (1,520 m)
Speed	57 mph (92 km/h)
Inversions	Two
Duration	3 min 40 sec

Four trains of six cars (three max. in use). Riders two x two rows; twenty-four riders per train

"Twisted Colossus," a steel roller coaster at Six Flags Magic Mountain amusement park, is a redevelopment of the original "Colossus" which first opened as a wooden coaster on June 29, 1978. After thirty-six years of successful operation, it was withdrawn from service: then, shortly after this was declared to be permanent, Six Flags revealed that it was going to be transformed by Rocky Mountain Construction to become "Twisted Colossus."

It reopened under its new name with a steel track and many other changes on May 23, 2015. "Twisted Colossus" has eighteen airtime hills, a zero-G roll where the track twists through 360 degrees, and a maneuver called a "High Five"—a feature where two trains pass through an overbanked turn while facing each other, which gives the illusion that you can reach out and "high five" the riders on the other track.

2015: "Baron 1898," Kaatsheuvel, Netherlands

Status	Operating
Opening date	July 1, 2015
Type	Steel dive
Cost	Approx. $20 million
Manufacturer	Bolliger & Mabillard
Lift/launch system	Chain lift hill
Height	98 ft (30 m)
Drop	123 ft (37.5 m)
Length	1,644 ft (501 m)
Speed	90 km/h (56 mph)
Inversions	Two
Duration	130 sec

Three trains of three cars. Riders six x one row; eighteen riders per train

"Baron 1898"— located at the Efteling theme park—is a double inversion, steampunk-style coaster themed around a nineteenth-century haunted Dutch gold mine. It dramatizes the mythical tale of greedy mine baron Gustave Hooghmoed, who discovered a system of old tunnels underneath Efteling just before the turn of the century. The ride designers visited real mines to give their vision authenticity— apart from a 90-degree free-fall drop into a 130-foot deep mineshaft and zero-G roll corkscrew! The three trains are able to take 1,000 passengers an hour. Reviewers love the theming and preshows, although the ride is not quite as dramatic. Efteling itself is the fourth most visted park in Europe. Nearly 5.2 million people visited in 2017, its sixty-fifth year of operation, enjoying the thirty-five rides—including six roller coasters.

2016: "Valravn," Sandusky, OH

Status	Operating
Opening date	May 7, 2016
Type	Steel dive
Manufacturer	Bolliger & Mabillard
Lift/launch system	Chain lift hill
Height	223 ft (68 m)
Drop	214 ft (65 m)
Length	3,415 ft (1,041 m)
Speed	75 mph (121 km/h)
Inversions	Three
Duration	1 min 58 sec

Three trains of three cars. Riders eight x single row; twenty-four riders per train

"Valravn" is a floorless, steel dive coaster—one of Cedar Point's record-breaking seventy-one rides and one of the five over 200 ft in height. When it opened it took the place of two earlier rides and immediately set several records for being the tallest, fastest, and longest dive coaster in the world, with the longest drop, and the most inversions including the highest (at 165 ft). The name of the ride comes from Danish folklore and means "Raven of the slain," referring to the mythological bird that eats the flesh of warriors slain in battle. At night "Valravn's" lift hill is lit up with multicolored LEDs while the track is illuminated with white spotlights. 1,418,584 people enjoyed the ride in 2017.

2017: "Hydrus," Seaside Heights, NJ

Status	Operating
Opening date	May 26, 2017
Type	Steel Euro-fighter
Manufacturer	Gerstlauer
Designer	Werner Stengel
Height	72 ft (22 m)
Length	1,050 ft (320 m)
Speed	45 mph (72 km/h)
Inversions	Three

Two trains of one car. Riders four x two rows; eight riders per train

"Hydrus" is located at Casino Pier in Seaside Heights. It was built to replace a previous ride—"Star Jet," which was very badly damaged by Hurricane Sandy in 2012 and then left to rust away in the surf—this time the ride has been built over the beach. It was the first Euro-Fighter 320 in existence. At an angle of 97 degrees, its drop is past vertical which is characteristic for the model. At night "Hydrus" stands out, the neon green and bright blue track lit up. The new ride cost an undisclosed amount to build and was part of a general refurbishment of the park and Seaside Heights area.

2017: "Taron," Brühl, Germany

Status	Operating
Opening date	June 30, 2016
Type	Steel launched
Manufacturer	Intamin
Lift/launch system	LSM
Length	4,593 ft (1,400 m)
Speed	72 mph (116 km/h)

Four trains of four cars. Riders two x two rows: sixteen riders per train

"Taron" is a multilaunch steel roller coaster that opened on June 30, 2016, and is located at Phantasialand in Germany. It runs through a themed world called Klugheim that has a rocky basalt landscape with a rustic village at its heart. The detailing of the surroundings is so good and the structure so solid, that the entire ride is a thoroughly smooth and enjoyable experience. Manufactured by Intamin, it is of the linear synchronous motor (LSM) launch type which helps it achieve its maximum speed of 72 mph. Although it has no inversions, the track has 58 intersecting points which allow it to cross over itself 116 times in a single run, which in itself is a world record. It replaced an earlier ride called "Silvermine."

2017: "Wicker Man," Alton Towers, UK

"Wicker Man" is the first wooden roller coaster to be built in the UK for over twenty years, but its old-school charm is updated with cutting-edge special effects designed to provide the most immersive thrill ride yet. The build and took 500,000 man-hours to build after four years in development. The ride is themed as a ritual by the pagan "Beornen" peoples who pay tribute with human sacrifices—the riders are their offering—to the Wicker Man who rules their land. Riders are then sent into a secretive world via a twisting labyrinthine track, dodging flames, smoke, and embers as it goes, with the Wicker Man bursting into flames as the train passes through. Along the way it travels through two smoky, flame-filled tunnels, drops three times, and passes through the Wicker Man three times, all to spectacular light, smoke, and flame effects. Despite appearances, no wood is burned around the track.

Status	Operating
Opening date	March 20, 2018
Type	Wooden sit down
Cost	£16 million
Manufacturer	Great Coasters International
Designer	Jeff Pike
Length	2,027.5 ft (51.5 m)
Drop	72.2 ft (22 m)
Speed	44 mph (71 km/h)
Duration	3 min 30 sec

Trains of twelve cars. Riders 2 x one row, twenty-four riders per train

2018: "Valkyria," Liseberg, Gothenburg, Sweden

Named after the mythical Norse Valkyries who carry fallen heroes to the afterlife in Valhalla, "Valkyria" is the longest and highest steel dive coaster in Europe. Mimicking the swooping flight of the mythical female creatures, this custom-built, floorless, steel dive coaster delivers a stomach-lurching vertical drop of 164 ft and then an immediate plunge into an underground smoke-filled tunnel at over 65 mph. Classified as an extreme ride, it also includes three inversions—an Immelmann,

a heartline roll, and a zero-G roll. The entire experience is heavily Nordic-themed with swords and shields and Norse decorations as well as naturalistic elements like stone, fire, and wood.

The ride is located in the myths and legends themed area of the largest amusement park in Scandinavia, and replaced an earlier ride called "Kanonen" that closed in December 2016. Nearby is a 40-rider pendulum ride constructed by Intamin named "Loke."

Status	Operating
Opening date	2019
Type	Floorless dive coaster
Manufacturer	Bollinger & Mabillard
Lift/launch system	Chain lift hill
Height	154.2 ft (46.5 m)
Length	2,460 ft (750 m)
Speed	65 mph (105 kph)
Duration	1 min 30 sec

Three trains of three cars. Riders six x one row: 18 riders per train

After a year of ground works, construction of the track itself started at the beginning of 2018. Problems with the tunnel delayed the opening from the first day of the 2018 season to August 10, 2018.

Left Just as the train is about to go over the edge the cars pause, and passengers are suspended in the air for a couple of seconds to look down at the terrifying drop into the underground. They then plummet vertically 164 feet (50 m) into an underground tunnel at a speed of around 65 mph (105 kph).

2019: "Steel Curtain," Kennywood, West Mifflin, PA

Status	Operating
Opening date	Summer 2019
Type	Hyper coaster
Manufacturer	S&S–Sansei Technologies
Lift/launch system	Chain lift hill
Height	215 ft (65.5 m)
Length	4,000 ft (1,219 m)
Speed	76 mph (122 kph)
Inversions	Nine
Duration	110 sec
G-Force	4 Gs

Two trains of six cars. Riders two x two row: 24 riders per train

"Steel Curtain" is decked out in the Pittsburgh Steelers distinctive black and gold colors and is designed to be an intense, inversion-filled coaster featuring the world's tallest inversion at a stomach turning 197 feet. This is just one of nine inversions (including a banana roll), the most in North America!

The ride sits in a new fan zone called Steelers Country dedicated to local American football heroes Pittsburgh Steelers and contains a variety of football related activities and restaurant. The ride uniquely features an airtime hill with a zero-G fall called "Top Gun" that riders experience upside down! Its name comes from the nickname given to the Pittsburgh Steelers' defensive line during the 1970s when the team won the Super Bowl four times in six years.

Above "Steel Curtain" replaced an earlier ride called "Log Jammer." Developed and built under the code name "Project 412," this latest record-breaking ride is certain to be a fan favorite.

Chapter Seven: Manufacturers

This section examines a few of the many manufacturers of thrill rides. Over the years they have produced many different types of roller coastes, many of which have been discussed earlier.

Below This is "Sky Wheel" at Allgäu Skyline Park, Bad Woerishofen, Germany. Opened in 2004, it was built by Maurer Söhne and is one of ten "Skyloop" steel coasters built by the company (nine XT 150s—as here—and one XT 450).

Arrow Development / Arrow Dynamics

Arrow Development was a company that designed and built amusement rides and roller coasters, starting in 1945 and going through a series of owners until its demise in 1981. It was then taken over by Arrow-Huss, followed by Arrow Dynamics.

Over the years, Arrow Development manufactured around 200 different thrill rides, including corkscrews, looping coasters, mine trains, log flumes, and automotive models. When the company became Arrow Dynamics, it moved from California to Utah where it produced many well known rides before closing in 2001. The company is now owned by Sansei Technologies, formerly S&S Worldwide.

Left "The Big One" at Blackpool Pleasure Beach, an Arrow Dynamics steel roller coaster that opened in 1994.

Bolliger & Mabillard Inc.

Bolliger & Mabillard Consulting Engineers Inc., to give the company its full title, was founded by Walter Bolliger and Claude Mabillard in 1998, and is based in Monthey, Switzerland. Essentially, the company comes up with the designs, while Clermont Steel Fabricators in Ohio, USA have done the manufacturing ever since 1990.

"B&M" for short, they have a first class reputation and have built over a hundred rides in their time, many of which introduced ground-breaking technologies.

Bolliger & Mabillard Inc.
Chemin des Dailles 31
CH-1870 Monthey
SWITZERLAND

http://www.bolliger-mabillard.com/

Left "Behemoth" is one of Bolliger & Mabillard most-loved designs and continues to be a crowd pleaser at Canada's Wonderland a decade after it opened in 2008. A hypercoaster, handled with great efficiency by the park to allow in ecess of 1,500 visitors an hour, it reaches 78 mph (125 km/h) in 3.9 seconds and has great airtime.

Dinn Corporation

The Dinn Corporation was a company that was founded in 1983 by Charles Dinn to design and manufacture roller coasters. Formed in West Chester Township, Butler County, Ohio, it became well known for relocating and refurbishing existing rides before it started building them outright. Ten such roller coasters were built, with more still on the drawing board before an acrimonious situation developed in 1991 over the construction of a new attraction called "Pegasus" at Efteling. The discord led Charles Dinn to close the corporation. Many of the key staff then joined Dinn's daughter Denise Dinn Larrick at her new venture, Custom Coasters International.

Right "Mean Streak" was a Dinn Corporation roller coaster that opened on May 11, 1991 at Cedar Point, Sandusky, Ohio.(See also p. 127.)

Gerstlauer

Gerstlauer Elektro GmbH—usually known simply as "Gerstlauer," was founded 1982 by Hubert Gerstlauer to make parts for his previous employers, roller coaster manufacturers Schwarzkopf GmbH. After they closed down, he bought some of their production facilities and took on the task of building amusement rides. He started with a bobsled coaster, but since then he has developed several different models. A good example is the Euro-Fighter range of roller coasters, which are now found all over the world—their signature attribute being "past vertical" drops. The Gerstlauer spinning roller coaster is also very popular.

Gerstlauer Amusement Rides GmbH,
Industriestrasse 17, D-86505 Münsterhausen,
Germany.
www.gerstlauer-rides.de

Right "Saw–The Ride" is a Gerstlauer Euro-Fighter thrill ride located at Thorpe Park, UK. (See also p. 170.)

Hopkins Rides

Hopkins Rides started out in 1962 manufacturing equipment like ski lifts, before moving over to focus on water rides and roller coasters in 1980. Although six of the seven coasters they built were for parks in the USA, such as their first construction called "Texas Tornado" at Wonderland Park in Texas, their last one in 1996 was "New Wild Mouse Coaster" at Misaki Park, Japan.

The company got into financial difficulties at the end of the 20th century, and was later relaunched as Hopkins Rides LLC in May 2002. They were then taken over by WhiteWater West, a water slide manufacturer, but still make water rides under the name Hopkins Rides.

Manufacturer Contact Details: Whitewater Attractions, 6700 McMillan Way, Richmond BC V6W 1J7, Canada
Phone: +1 604 273 1068
www.whitewaterwest.com

Left "Dragon" is a Hopkins Rides steel roller coaster located at Adventureland in Altoona, Iowa.

Intamin

Intamin Worldwide is a company that designs and builds thrill rides. It was founded in 1967, and has its headquarters in Wollerau, Switzerland, but it also has several other offices elsewhere including two in Europe, three in Asia, and two in the United States.

Intamin Worldwide produces 22 different kinds of rides, and has installed over 70 complete amusement park attractions. Intamin have often been the first to introduce new technologies or designs such as the linear synchronous motor (LSM) and hydraulic launch systems, as well as the ZacSpin, a type of fourth-dimension roller coaster.

Intamin AG, Verenastrasse 37, P.O. Box 95, CH-8832 Wollerau, Switzerland

T. +41-44-786 91 11
F. +41-44-785 02 02
info@intaminworldwide.com
www.intaminworldwide.com

Left "Kirnu"—is an Intamin ZacSpin roller coaster, at Linnanmäki in Finland.

Pinfari

Pinfari was a roller coaster manufacturer that operated out of Lombardy in Italy. Its first ride was called "Hochbahn" which opened at the Wiener Prater in Austria in 1966.

They made many different kinds of rides, with their model range including the Zyklon non-looping and looping coasters, the RC (an updated Zyklon), the Mini Mega M29 (a reduced size version of the RC), the Big Apple M28 (a caterpillar ride), the Queen Bee (an inverted kiddie coaster), the Xpress 56 (an inverted ride aimed at the travelling market), and the Super Dragon (a larger version of the Big Apple). Despite the success of these rides, Pinfari was a victim of the global recession, and it closed down in 2004.

Pinfari, Via Curtatone e Montanara 30/a, Suzzara, Lombardy 46029, Italy.
Tel: +39 0376 535 010
www.roller-coaster.it/

Left "Klondike Gold Mine," was a Pinfari ZL42 coaster, originally built at Drayton Manor, UK.

Premier Rides

Premier Rides, which designs and manufactures a variety of thrill rides including roller coasters, water rides, drop, tilt, and observation towers, was founded in 1994 in Maryland.

Their entry into this market was through the construction of two identical rides which opened on the same day—June 18, 1996. These were "Flight of Fear" at Kings Dominion in Virginia and at Kings Island in Ohio—both were themed to the well known science fiction TV show The Outer Limits, but due to copyright problems the name for the ride was changed.

The company is noted for introducing Linear Induction Motors (LIM) to the roller coaster scene, and makes a wide variety of models such as the LIM Bowl Coaster, LIM Shuttle Loop Coaster, Triple LIM Launch Coaster, Sky Rocket II (a triple-launch coaster), and the Liquid Coaster. They also build custom LSM Launch Coasters to order.

Premier Rides, 1007 East Pratt Street, Baltimore, Maryland 21202, USA
Tel.: +1 410 923 0414
Email: info@premierrides.com

www.premier-rides.com

Left Aerial view of "Back Lot Stunt" coaster, a ride themed to the movie **The Italian Job**, and built by Premier Rides.

Reverchon

Reverchon is a French company that mainly specializes in building spinning wild mouse coasters and water rides. They started out in the 1920s building bumper cars, but in the 1970s broadened out into constructing amusement park attractions. This spread to include roller coasters in the 1990s, with the first one—"Tigre de Sibérie"—located at Le Pal in France.

The mainstay of Reverchon production was the Crazy Mouse, a wild mouse coaster, of which many examples were built, including "Primeval Whirl," seen here. The company went into liquidation in September 2008, but has since been revived.

123 ZI Gaston Reverchon, 77920 Samois Sur Seine, France
0033 1 60 74 94 00

www.reverchon-attraction.com

Right Although it has moved three times "Famous Jack" is a very popular spinning-car ride of the wild mouse type. It is currently at Bagatelle, Merlimont, Hauts-de-France, France.

Rocky Mountain Construction

Rocky Mountain Construction is a manufacturing and construction company that is located in Hayden, Idaho. Formed in 2001, they have expanded ever since, and now have an impressive list of rides to their name, including "Iron Rattler," "Outlaw Run," "Goliath," "Twisted Colossus," and many, many others. One of these is "New Texas Giant" at Six Flags Over Texas, which was designed by Alan Schilke. This was the first roller coaster to feature their new I-Box track which was developed especially for wooden roller coasters. The company is thriving, and currently has several more rides under construction.

Rocky Mountain Construction
11470 Carisa Ct. Hayden, ID, USA 83835
208.772.8181

www.rockymtnconstruction.com

Right "Iron Rattler" is a steel roller coaster manufactured by Rocky Mountain Construction and located at Six Flags Fiesta Texas.

S&S—Sansei Technologies

Like so many thrill ride manufacturers, S&S Worldwide has a complicated history. These days the company is known as Sansei Technologies, however, it started out in 1989 when it mostly made amusement equipment.

Their first ride was "Space Shot," which they constructed in 1994. They renamed themselves S&S Power, a label under which they then operated until 2010, when they became S&S Worldwide. This version of the company then bought out the remains of Arrow Dynamics in 2002 after it went bankrupt, renaming themselves yet again—this time to S&S Arrow.

The core staff established themselves as experts in the use of pneumatics, and this capability allowed them to create such famous rides of which "Powder Keg: A Blast in the Wilderness" is just one of many. Sansei Yusoki of Japan bought a major share in the organisation, which then became known as S&S–Sansei Technologies.

S&S – Sansei Technologies Inc., 350 West 2500 North, Logan, UT 84341, USA
Phone: +1 435 752 1987

www.engineeringexcitement.com

Left "Steel Hawg," an S&S Worldwide roller coaster at Indiana Beach, Monticello, Indiana.

Vekoma

Vekoma is one of the world's main designers and manufacturers of thrill rides, and in its time has made over 300 of them, more than any other company. Based out of The Netherlands, they started out in 1926 in the agricultural market, but moved into this arena in 1967. Since then, they have been responsible for producing many different types of ride—including corkscrew and family boomerang roller coasters, suspended looping coasters (SLC), suspended family coasters, Vekoma launch coasters, flying Dutchmen, mine trains, water rides, and many others.

Vekoma Rides Manufacturing B.V., Schaapweg 18, 6063 BA Vlodrop, The Netherlands. Tel: +31 475 409 222

www.vekoma.com

Left "Blue Tornado," a steel inverted roller coaster that operates at Gardaland, near Verona, Italy.

Zamperla

Zamperla Spa is an Italian engineering company that has a long history within the amusement industry. It has a manufacturing base in Vicenza, Italy, but also has offices in the USA. Although it had been building thrill rides for many years, it really became established on the world scene when it produced seven rides for Walt Disney's amusement park Euro Disney, near Paris.

Zamperla have maintained their relationship with Disney, as well as with many other major organizations such as MCA Universal Studios, Paramount, Six Flags, and Warner Bros. They produce many different off-the-shelf models, such as the Thunderbolt, Volare, the Family Gravity Coaster, and the Powered Coaster.

Zamperla S.p.A. Italy, Via Monte Grappa, 15/17, I-36077 Altavilla Vicentina (VI).
Phone: +39 0444 998400
email: zamperla@zamperla.it

www.zamperla.com

Right Zamperla roller coaster "Thunderbolt," a big attraction and looking good at Coney Island.

Zierer

Zierer is a German company that manufactures family friendly amusement rides, with about 130 of their coasters currently being used worldwide. They have a wide range of types on offer, although their first, the Flitzer has been discontinued, and the Tivoli has been replaced by a newer model. There are, however, lots of others, including the tower launch coaster, the tower speed coaster, the drop element coaster, the elevated seating coaster, and another simply known as force. Other attractions they produce range from Ferris wheels to drop towers, to monorails, and various water rides.

Zierer Karussell-und Spezial-maschinenbau GmbH & Co. KG, Josef-Wallner-Straße 5, 94469 Deggendorf
Phone: +49 (0)991 91060
www.zierer.com/

Right "Kikkerachtbaan," which translates as "Frog Roller Coaster" was built by Zierer and is located in the Dutch amusement park Duinrell.

Index of Rides